So you really want to learn

Junior English

Book 2

GALORE PARK

So you really want to learn

Junior English

Book 2

Andrew Hammond MA

Series Editor: Susan Elkin MA BA (Hons) Cert Ed

www.galorepark.co.uk

Published by Galore Park Publishing Ltd
19/21 Sayers Lane, Tenterden, Kent TN30 6BW
www.galorepark.co.uk

Design, layout and typography Design Gallery, Suffolk
Illustrations by Gwyneth Williamson and Rosie Brooks

Printed by Replika Press Pvt. Ltd., India

ISBN: 978 1 902984 81 0

First published 2007, reprinted 2008, 2010, autumn 2010, 2011.

An answer book is available to accompany this book:
ISBN 978 1 902984 86 5

Details of other Galore Park publications are available at www.galorepark.co.uk

ISEB Revision Guides, publications and examination papers may also be obtained from Galore Park.

The publishers are grateful for permission to use the extracts and photographs as follows:

Extract from 'Snow White', A Kaleidoscope of Fairies and Fables re-told by Robert Mathias (Hamlyn, 1988), pp.110-2 permission sought; extract from
'Snow facts', source www.richardjwild.co.uk © Richard J. Wild 2007, reproduced by kind permission of the author; extract from 'A heavenly holiday',
source www.atlantistravel.co.uk © Atlantis Travel Group 2007, reproduced by kind permission of the Atlantis Travel Group; extract from 'Kensuke's
Kingdom', abridged from Kensuke's Kingdom by Michael Morpurgo (Heinemann, 1999), pp.49-52 copyright © Michael Morpurgo 1999, reproduced by
kind permission of the agents David Higham Associates; extract from 'Inside the giant peach', Roald Dahl's James and the Giant Peach: A Play adapted
by Richard R. George (Puffin, 1982), pp.25-7 permission sought; extract from 'A surprising find', Brilliant the Dinosaur by Richard Stilgoe (Pavilion Books,
1994), pp.18-20 copyright © Richard Stilgoe 1994, reproduced by kind permission of Pavilion (Anova) Children's Books; extract from 'The long-necked
beast', Eyewitness Guides: Dinosaur by David Norman and Angela Milner (Dorling Kindersley, 1989), pp.14-5 copyright © Dorling Kindersley Ltd 1989,
reproduced by kind permission of Penguin Books Ltd; extract from 'Steaming ahead', All About Trains edited by Michael Harris (Southwater, 2001),
pp.4-5, 8 copyright © Anness Publishing Ltd 2001, reproduced by kind permission of Anness Publishing Ltd; extract from 'Circus elephant', A Trunkful
of Elephants edited by Judith Nicholls (Methuen, 1994), pp.56-7 copyright © Judith Nicholls 1994, permission sought; extract from 'Wolf', Dragonsfire
by Judith Nicholls (Faber and Faber, 1990), p.14 copyright © Judith Nicholls 1990, reproduced by kind permission of the author; extract from 'Precious
animals', source www.wwf.org.uk/gowild/planet.htm © WWF 2000, reproduced by kind permission of the WWF; extract from 'Stig of the dump', Stig of
the Dump by Clive King (Puffin, 1963), pp.4-8 copyright © Clive King 1963, reproduced by kind permission of Penguin Books Ltd; extract from 'Crusty
crab', Look Closer: Rock Pool by Christine Gunzi (Dorling Kindersley, 1992), p.14 copyright © Dorling Kindersley 1992, reproduced by kind permission
of Penguin Books Ltd; extract from 'Together at last', The Silver Sword by Ian Serraillier (Jonathan Cape, 1956), pp.151-3 copyright © Ian Serraillier 1956,
reproduced by kind permission of The Random House Group Ltd; extract from 'Brave Anne', The Diary of Anne Frank (Pan Books, 1954), p.136 copyright
© Anne Frank Foundation, reproduced by kind permission of the Anne Frank Foundation; extract from 'The iron man', The Iron Man by Ted Hughes
(Faber and Faber 1968), pp.11-3 copyright © Ted Hughes 1968, reproduced by kind permission of Faber and Faber Ltd; extract from 'The obedient
robot', source www.bbc.co.uk/wales/southwest/sites/mystory, article © Clare Wojciechowski 2007, reproduced by kind permission of the author.

Photo credits: P17 Sebastian Szlasa, P28 Top Kim Taylor © Dorliing Kindersley, Bottom Colin Keates © Dorling Kindersley, Courtesy of the Natural History
Museum, London, P50 © Dorling Kindersley, P63 © John Cancalosi / Alamy, P75 Rafael Macia / Science Photo Library, P84 Frank Greenaway © Dorling
Kindersley, Courtesy of the Natural History Museum, London, P96 Getty Images

Acknowledgements

My thanks go to the students, staff and parents around me who have, in their own ways, helped me in preparing this second volume in the *Junior English* series.

Thanks also to Susan Elkin and Nick Oulton for their continued editorial support. It is a pleasure to work for such similar pedants for punctuation and sticklers for style.

Finally my thanks to Andrea, Henry, Nell and young Edward for their continued patience while Daddy writes his books.

A.J.H.

Preface

This is the second volume in the three-part series of *Junior English*, which, I hope, serves as a fitting prequel to the much acclaimed *So You Really Want to Learn English* series by Susan Elkin.

In choosing the texts, writing the questions and preparing the wide range of related tasks that follow each excerpt, I have tried, at all times, to offer readers an enjoyable and stimulating mix of old and new, whilst maintaining the quality and rigour you would expect from a prep school resource. The National Curriculum, the National Literacy Strategy and the new Core Learning Skills of the Primary Framework all play their part in this collection, but they do not eclipse the stalwarts of prep school education, namely Common Entrance, creativity and some good old-fashioned common sense.

I hope that through this, and the other titles in the series, the teaching and learning of English in your classroom continues to be a hugely beneficial and fun experience for pupil and pedant.

A.J.H.

Contents

Introduction..1

Chapter 1..3

Snow White..3
Snow facts (www.richardjwild.co.uk)..5
Learning about language...7
      Common and proper nouns...7
      Word order 8
Can you spell?...10
      Words to show gender..10
Speaking and listening..11
Have you read?..12
Other things to do...12

Chapter 2..14

Lost in paradise (*Kensuke's Kingdom*)..14
A heavenly holiday (www.atlantistravel.co.uk)..16
Learning about language...19
      Adjectives..19
      Types of sentence...20
Can you spell?...21
      Similar letters, different sounds...21
Speaking and listening..23
Have you read?..24
Other things to do...24

Chapter 3..25

Inside the giant peach (*James and the Giant Peach*)..25
Lots of legs...28
Learning about language...30
      Verbs..30
      Exclamation marks 31
Can you spell?...33
      Common endings (*-ible*, *-able*)...33
Speaking and listening..34
Have you read?..35
Other things to do...35

Chapter 4..36

A surprising find (*Brilliant the Dinosaur*)..............................36
The long-necked beast 38
Learning about language..40
      Missing letters (apostrophes 1)..40
      Its and it's..42
Can you spell?..43
      Big, bigger, biggest...43
Speaking and listening...45
Have you read?...45
Other things to do...46

Chapter 5..47

The Railway Children..47
Steaming ahead (*All About Trains*) 50
Learning about language..53
      Personal pronouns 53
      Simple sentences..56
Can you spell?..57
      Prefixes and suffixes..57
Speaking and listening...59
Have you read?...60
Other things to do...60

Chapter 6..61

'Circus elephant'; 'Wolf'...61
Precious animals...62
Learning about language..65
      Possessive pronouns..65
      Belonging to... (apostrophes 2) 66
Can you spell?..68
      Collective nouns...68
Speaking and listening...69
Have you read?...70
Other things to do...70

Chapter 7 71

Stig of the Dump 71
Waste 74
Learning about language 77
    Speech marks 77
    Imperatives 79
Can you spell? 80
    i before *e* 80
Speaking and listening 81
Have you read? 82
Other things to do 82

Chapter 8 83

'Crabs Walk Sideways' 83
Crusty crab 84
Learning about language 86
    Alliteration 86
    Prepositions 87
Can you spell? 89
    More common endings (-*en*, -*on*) 89
Speaking and listening 90
Have you read? 91
Other things to do 92

Chapter 9 93

Together at last (*The Silver Sword*) 93
Brave Anne (*The Diary of Anne Frank*) 97
Learning about language 99
    Adverbs 99
    Capital letters 100
Can you spell? 102
    -*sion* and -*tion* 102
Speaking and listening 103
Have you read? 104
Other things to do 104

Chapter 10..105

The Iron Man...105
The Obedient Robot...107
Learning about language...110
      Similes...110
      Compound sentences....................................112
Can you spell?..113
      Adding the letters –ing................................113
Speaking and listening...115
Have you read?..115
Other things to do...116

"And anyway, there is nothing marvellous, you know, Centipede, about having a lot of legs."

From Roald Dahl's James and the Giant Peach

Introduction

Inside this small book there hides a talking Diplodocus, a giant peach, a circus elephant and an iron man. You will be welcomed onto a desert island paradise, hauled through giant snowdrifts, invited onto a rubbish dump and whisked away on a green dragon, first class.

Where else would you find so many different delights than in a book? Such is the beauty of reading.

There will be questions too. Some will probably make you grumpy, confused or frustrated. But there will be others that make you leap up and laugh, because you know the answer. You may be asked to write stories, newspaper articles, letters, diaries and play scripts. These tasks provide golden opportunities to have some fun with words, and show your teachers what you can really do. You may even be asked to perform plays, improvise with friends, give presentations and join in class debates.

So many different tasks. But they all share the same goals: to help you to use language more successfully and to remind you that learning English can be fun! Weighed down by worksheets on grammar, punctuation and spelling, especially on a rainy Monday, you could be forgiven for thinking that English is dull. But it's not. In fact it is far from dull, so far from the planet Dull that you could barely see it with the naked eye. English is exciting, surprising, amusing, baffling even, but it's never dull.

English is about using language to express what is in your mind. The good news is you've been doing that for longer than you think. From the moment you were born, in fact, you began finding ways of communicating what you need and what you want to those around you, and you've continued to express yourself ever since.

The problem comes when someone points out, rather unhelpfully you think, that you can't spell *crocodile*. And you must not begin a sentence with *and*. Or you've committed the worst sin of all, by contracting some words with an apostrophe in a formal sentence. Now you've done it!

It is true that English can be difficult. There are so many rules and lessons to learn, and for every rule there seems to be an exception. But, whatever you do, don't think that you CAN'T DO English. You CAN. You are 'doing' English every day.

Read the passages, have a go at the questions and do your best in the writing tasks. Enjoy improving your speaking and listening – these are *very* important skills – and find time to explore some of the 'other things to do'. Use your imagination whenever you can. But most importantly…

… keep reading!

A.J.H.

Chapter 1

Snow White

It was the middle of winter and broad flakes of snow were tumbling and swirling around in the cold night air. Dark shadows crept into every nook and cranny and stood out sharply against the pale silver glow reflected from the moonlit snowdrifts. The small creatures of the forest had taken
5 refuge, huddling deep in their nests far below the frozen shroud that lay across the land.

High on a hill above the ice-latticed treetops stood a castle. It rested like a great black rock amidst the gleaming whiteness that surrounded it. Its turrets and walls were dark and gloomy in the creaking chill, blind save
10 for a solitary golden glow high up in one corner of its ebony facade. The glow came from a tiny window and it flickered like a dying star as the snowflakes danced past it.

Close by the window sat a queen quietly sewing and looking out
15 over the frosty scene. She had a child within her whose birth was near, but despite the joy this brought her, there was a sadness in her heart. As she measured
20 her stitches she prayed for strength, for the cold of the long winter had entered her bones and she felt frail and weak.

Suddenly, she started, as the
25 sharp needle pierced her finger and three drops of blood fell on to the snow-covered windowsill. She gazed thoughtfully at the crimson stains colouring the
30 white snow and her sad eyes filled with tears.

'Would that my child be a daughter with skin as white as that snow, with cheeks as rosy red as blood and hair as ebony black as the window-frame.'

35 Outside the wind gusted wildly and the long night wore on.

The good queen died but her child was, indeed, a daughter. The queen had died that the child should live, but just before she closed her eyes for the last time she saw that her wish had come true – the child's skin was as fair as driven snow, her cheeks were rosy blood-red and her shining
40 hair was as black as ebony. The queen's lips had trembled; 'I will call her Snow White,' she murmured.

(From Snow White by The Brothers Grimm, re-told by Robert Mathias, 1986)

· ·

Exercise 1.1

Read the passage from *Snow White* and then answer the following questions in complete sentences.

1. Write a word or phrase that shows it is night time at the beginning of the story.

2. How do the forest creatures keep warm during the cold, snowy winter?

3. How can you tell, from the outside, that there is someone in the castle?

4. What gave the queen a sudden shock?

5. The queen wishes for a daughter with pale skin, red cheeks and shiny black hair. Where did she get these ideas from?

6. Do you think the atmosphere in this story would have been different if it had been set in summer time? Explain your answer as fully as you can in a few sentences.

7. Use a dictionary to find the meanings of the following words: (a) *nook* (line 2); (b) *refuge* (line 5); (c) *gusted* (line 35); (d) *murmured* (line 41).

Snow facts

The snowiest winter in Great Britain was in 1947. Between 22nd January and 17th March snow fell every day somewhere across the UK.

Permanent snow and ice covers about 12% of the Earth's land surface, a total of around 21 million square kilometres.

5 A single snowstorm can drop 40 million tons of snow, carrying energy equivalent to 120 atom bombs.

The largest snowflake ever measured fell across Fort Keogh in Montana, U.S.A. on 28th January 1887. It measured 38cm across and was 20cm thick.

The worst blizzards are in Antarctica, where wind speeds can reach up to 10 193km / hour.

The world record for the highest amount of snow to fall in a single winter season was 2,896cm (nearly 30 metres) between November 1998 and June 1999 on Mount Baker, Washington State, U.S.A.

On 3rd November 1958, rain fell on 34th Street, New York City, while 15 guards at the top of the Empire State Building at 350m were making snowballs.

Snow fell in Riyadh, Saudi Arabia, on 1st January 1973.

(From the website of Dr Richard J. Wild at www.richardjwild.co.uk)

Exercise 1.2 ✏

Read the passage entitled 'Snow facts' and then answer the following questions in complete sentences.

1. What percentage of the Earth's surface is ice or permanent snow?

2. How much snow can fall in a single snow storm?

3. The largest snowflake ever recorded fell in Montana, U.S.A. in 1887. How big was it?

4. What was so surprising about the weather conditions in New York on 3rd November 1958?

5. Why would it have been surprising to see snow in Riyadh, Saudi Arabia?

6. Write the meanings of the following words, using a dictionary to help you: (a) *permanent* (line 3); (b) *equivalent* (line 6); (c) *blizzard* (line 9); (d) *website* (line 18).

Exercise 1.3

Your turn to write:

1. Read the passage entitled *Snow White* again. Continue the story in your own words. You could use what you know about the traditional story of Snow White or you might want to create a new adventure for her.

2. Write a short description of a beautiful place, such as a forest or a hillside, when it is covered in freshly laid snow.

3. Do you like to play in the snow? If you do, what do you like about it especially? Why do so many people love playing in the snow too? Why do we find it so magical? Write about your feelings. If you do not enjoy being outside in the snow, then explain what it is you don't like.

4. Write a poem in which the word 'SNOWFLAKE' appears down the left hand side and each letter begins the first word of each line. This is called an **acrostic** poem. So, for instance:

COLD

Colour blue, icy and crisp
Outside in the snow
Lakes, rivers, puddles frozen
Dark evenings by a glowing fire.

Learning about language

Common and proper nouns

A noun is the name of a person, place or thing:

Person	Place	Thing
David	Manchester	table
Dr Richard Wild	New York	snow

Notice that the names of persons and places begin with a capital letter. This is because they are proper names. So we call them **proper nouns**. Ordinary things (**table**, **snow**) are called **common nouns**.

Common nouns are everywhere. Every time you touch something you are probably touching a thing which has a common noun for its name – like **ball**, **desk** or **car**.

. . . .

Exercise 1.4

Copy the following sentences, underlining the common nouns in each. There may be more than one.

1. The snowflakes fell gently onto the cold stones.

2. Her eyes filled with tears.

3. The sharp needle pierced her finger.

4. About 12% of the surface of the Earth is covered in snow and ice.

5. The largest snowflake landed in Montana in America.

Exercise 1.5 ✏️

Now copy the following sentences, adding capital letters to each proper noun.

1. The queen named her little child snow white.

2. The guards made snowballs high up on the empire state building.

3. The snowiest winter in great britain was in 1947.

4. Snow didn't usually fall in saudi arabia.

5. snow white had skin as pale as white snow.

· ·

Word order

In some languages the order of words in a sentence does not matter because the meaning stays the same. But in English it matters a great deal. If you rearrange words in an English sentence you may get entirely the wrong meaning.

Look at these examples:

The snowflakes fell on the little girl.
The little girl fell on the snowflakes.

The queen called the little girl Snow White.
The girl called the little queen Snow White.

The usual order for a sentence is:

The	*snowflakes*	*covered*	*the little girl*
	subject	**verb**	**object**

If you change the subject and the object around, it usually reverses the meaning. You will learn more about subject, verb and object in Chapter 5.

Exercise 1.6 🖋

In each of the following sentences the subject has changed places with the object, to make some peculiar meanings. Rewrite them as they were intended. You will need to change some capital letters too.

1. The letters delivered the postman.

2. Some apples ate my son.

3. Yesterday the dog took Michael for a walk.

4. The thief arrested the policeman and took him to the station for questioning.

5. Gran stung a wasp.

Exercise 1.7 🖋

The following sentences come from the passages above but they have been copied down incorrectly. Rewrite each one putting the words in the right order.

1. High on a castle stood treetops above the ice-latticed hill.

2. Close by the queen sat a frosty window quietly looking out over the scene and sewing.

3. Thoughtfully she gazed at the white snow colouring the tears and her sad eyes filled with crimson stains.

4. Her lips had trembled; 'I will call the queen Snow White,' she murmured.

5. The good daughter died but her queen was indeed a child.

Can you spell?

Words to show gender

Some nouns or 'naming words' can be sorted according to **gender**. By looking at them we can tell whether we are talking about a man or a woman. Look at the following examples:

brother   -   sister

father   -   mother

Words that refer to men are called **masculine** and those that refer to women are called **feminine**. Here are some more examples:

Masculine	Feminine
husband	wife
king	queen
man	woman

Exercise 1.8

Now see if you can complete the following table by adding the masculine or feminine nouns that are missing.

Masculine	Feminine
prince	
	actress
	aunt
groom	
	niece
lord	

Exercise 1.9 🖉

When the letters –ess appear at the end of a word, this often (though not always) suggests that the word is feminine. Which of these words have feminine equivalents? Copy these words into your book. Then decide which of them are gender nouns. Write the **feminine** versions next to the **masculine** words.

I. host

2. teacher

3. lion

4. child

5. tiger

6. headmaster

Speaking and listening

I. News report: Write the script for a short news presentation in which it is announced that snowstorms have struck Britain, leaving motorists stranded and electricity cables broken. Present this news report to your class. Remember to read it like a newsreader.

2. Role-play: Work in groups of three or four. Act out a scene in which you enjoy a skiing holiday together in the snowy mountains of France. Sadly, one of you becomes injured. How will you get this person off the slope to safety? What might happen on the way? Think about making your scene as exciting as possible for your audience. Then perform it for your class.

3. Interview: Imagine that Snow White is being interviewed for a job as a top fashion model. What sort of questions might she be asked by the panel of interviewers? What sort of answers might she give? Will she be pretty enough? Will she be tough enough to cope with the busy life of a model? Work in a group of about three and perform the job interview for your class.

4. Talking pairs: With a partner, perform a short role-play. One of you is an alien from another planet (who happens to speak English!). The other is an ordinary person from Earth. The alien has never seen snow before and wants to know what it is, so his or her partner describes it.

Have you read?

Here are some collections of famous fairy tales for you to enjoy.

The Usborne Book of Fairy Tales by Heather Amery (Usborne Publishing Ltd)
Princess Stories by Heather Amery (Usborne Publishing Ltd)
The Oxford Treasury of Fairy Tales by Geraldine McCaughrean (Oxford University Press)
Fairy Tales by Hans Christian Andersen (Penguin Classics)
The Complete Brothers Grimm Fairy Tales by Fairy Tale and Folklore (Gramercy Books)
The Golden Book of Fairy Tales by Adrienne Segur (Golden Books)
Children's Classic Stories by Anne Marshall (Miles Kelly Publishing Ltd)

And here are some unusual versions to make you laugh.

Snow White and the Seven Aliens by Laurence Anholt (Orchard Books)
12 Fabulously Funny Fairy Tale Plays by Justin McCory Martin (Instructor Books)
Cinderella Outgrows the Glass Slipper and other Zany Fractured Fairy Tale Plays by J. M. Wolf (Scholastic)
Roald Dahl's Revolting Rhymes by Roald Dahl (Puffin Books)

Other things to do...

- Working in small groups, choose a well-known fairy tale. Write and perform a short play version of the story. Think of the characters, the settings and the script. It doesn't have to be a long play – you may be able to tell the whole story in just a few minutes.

- Find the complete tale of Snow White. Then write your own version of the story, changing the characters and the setting to make it more modern. Snow White could be a pop star, and the seven dwarves could be her dancers, for example.

- Find out more about the fascinating subject of snow. Use the Internet, books and magazines to help you put together a 'Fascinating Factfile' which contains lots of interesting information, including, for example:

  - how Eskimos live

  - how a polar bear survives

  - some famous snow rescue stories

  - instructions on how to build an igloo

  - ideas for snow sculptures.

Chapter 2

Lost in paradise

For Michael, sailing around the world with his parents was a dream come true. Now he finds himself washed up on a strange island in the Pacific Ocean, tired and lonely.

'I sat up. I was on a beach, a broad white sweep of sand, with trees growing thick and lush behind me right down to the beach. Then I saw Stella prancing about in the shallows. I called her and she came bounding up out of the sea to greet me, her tail circling wildly. When all the leaping
5 and licking and hugging were done, I struggled to my feet.

I was weak all over. I looked all about me. The wide, blue sea was as empty as the cloudless sky above. No *Peggy Sue*. No boat. Nothing. No one. I called again and again for my mother and my father. I called until the tears came and I could call no more, until I knew there was no
10 point. I stood there for some time trying to work out how I had got here, how it was that I'd survived...

...Then came the howling again from the trees, and the hackles went up on Stella's neck. She charged up the beach barking and barking, until she was sure she had silenced the last of the echoes. It was a musical, plaintive
15 howling this time, not at all menacing. I thought I recognised it. I had heard howling like it once before on a visit to London Zoo. Gibbons, 'funky gibbons', my father had called them. I still don't know why to this day. But I loved the sound of the word 'funky'. Perhaps that was why I remembered what they were. 'It's only gibbons,' I told Stella, 'just funky gibbons. They
20 won't hurt us.' But I couldn't be at all sure I was right.

From where I now stood I could see that the forest grew more sparsely up the side of a great hill some way inland, and it occurred to me then that if I could reach the bare, rocky outcrop at the summit, I would be able to see further out to sea. Or perhaps there'd be some house or farm
25 further inland, or maybe a road, and I could find someone to help. But if I left the beach and they came back looking for me, what then? I decided I would have to take that chance.

I set off at a run, Stella Artois at my heels, and soon found myself in the cooling shade of the forest. I discovered a narrow track going uphill, in the
30 right direction, I thought. So I followed it, only slowing to a walk when the hill became too steep. The forest was alive with creatures. Birds cackled and screeched high above me, and always the howling wailed and wafted through the trees, but more distantly now.

It wasn't the sounds of the forest that bothered me, though, it was the
35 eyes. I felt as if I was being watched by a thousand inquisitive eyes. I think Stella did, too, for she had been strangely quiet ever since we entered the forest, constantly glancing up at me for reassurance and comfort. I did my best to give it, but she could sense that I, too, was frightened.

(From Kensuke's Kingdom by Michael Morpurgo, 1999)

Exercise 2.1 ✏️

Read the passage from *Kensuke's Kingdom* by Michael Morpurgo and then answer the following questions in complete sentences.

1. (a) Who, or what, do you think Stella is?

(b) Write a word or phrase that helped you to decide.

2. What was the name of Michael's boat?

3. What made the hackles on Stella's neck stand up?

4. Why did Michael want to climb to the rocky summit of the hill?

5. Do you think Michael is a brave boy? Write a sentence or two explaining your thoughts about how he reacts to the situation he is in.

6. Use a dictionary to find the meanings of the following words: (a) *hackles* (line 12); (b) *plaintive* (line 14); (c) *menacing* (line 15); (d) *sparsely* (line 21).

. . . .

A heavenly holiday

Fancy a holiday in paradise? David and Jill Gilmour believe they have the perfect destination for you.

Wakaya Club – Fiji

Described as heaven on earth, Wakaya Club's home is a small, far-flung, private Fijian island, surrounded by crystalline, coral-ringed lagoons, and fringed with soaring cliffs and shell-strewn beaches.

5 Just nine luxurious, cathedral-ceilinged cottages have been built as an extension to owners David and Jill Gilmour's island home, using natural woods and thatch. The Gilmours' private villa, Vale O, or 'house in the clouds' is said to be one of the finest in the South Pacific and is available to guests to experience when the owners are not in residence.

10 Make your way to the Palm Grove dining pavilion to the sound of Lali drums, where four resident chefs create sumptuous dishes, following the weekly Meke song and dance pageant featuring a traditional Lovo feast.

Explore the tribal archaeological sites or take a beach picnic to your own secluded cove. For energising pursuits play a round of golf, a set of tennis
15 or enjoy superb scuba diving.

Accommodation:
9 Bure Cottages – 1 Garden View, 7 Ocean View and a Governor's Bure

Facilities:
Restaurant, fitness bure, massage room, freshwater pool, snorkeling, 9-hole
20 'fun' golf course, tennis and croquet. Two scuba dives per person per day.

Location:
Wakaya Island, Fiji, 45 minutes flight from Nadi Airport by private plane.

Prices:
7 nights All-Inclusive in a Garden View Bure, flying Air New Zealand from
25 £5476 to £5809 per person (extra nights from £584).

(From the Atlantis Travel website at www.atlantistravel.co.uk)

Exercise 2.2 ✏

Read the passage entitled 'A heavenly holiday' and then answer the following questions in complete sentences.

1. Why do you think this island is described as 'heaven on earth'?

2. What do you understand by the phrase 'cathedral-ceilinged cottages'?

3. List some of the attractions in the Palm Grove dining pavilion.

4. Which of the following people could you recommend this type of holiday to, and why?

    (a) a family with teenage boys

    (b) an elderly couple with a fear of flying

    (c) a honeymoon couple

    (d) a group of rock climbers.

5. Would you like to visit the Wakaya Club resort? Give reasons to support your answer.

6. Use a dictionary to find the meanings of the following words: (a) *crystalline* (line 3); (b) *thatch* (line 7); (c) *sumptuous* (line 11); (d) *pageant* (line 12).

· ·

Exercise 2.3 ✏

Your turn to write:

1. Imagine, like Michael, that you have been washed up on a desert island, tired and lonely. What will you do for food and shelter? How will you survive? How will you attract the attention of passing ships? Write a short story entitled 'Shipwrecked in Paradise'.

2. Imagine you are Michael, stranded on the island. When you were washed overboard, you had a bag of possessions with you. You managed to hold onto it whilst in the water. Now, safely on the beach, you find some paper and a pencil inside, and a bottle of lemonade. You decide to write an 'SOS' message on the paper, place it in the bottle and send it out to sea for someone to find. Write this message.

3. Do you think that remote island paradises, like the one that is home to the Wakaya Club, should be left to the villagers and the wildlife that live there? Or do you think that the visiting tourists bring some much-needed cash to the region? Write about the advantages and disadvantages of turning quiet paradises into holiday resorts.

Learning about language
Adjectives

In the first passage above, the sea is described as **wide** and **blue**, and the sky is **cloudless**. These words describe the sea and the sky for us. Sometimes we call them describing words, but their real name is **adjectives**.

An adjective adds extra meaning to the noun, or naming word. It tells us more about how the noun looks, sounds, feels, smells or tastes. So, for example, we might have:

dazzling sunshine   or   **soft** sand

Exercise 2.4

Write the following sentences and underline the adjective in each one.

1. I was washed up on a deserted island.

2. I could hear the soft sound of the sea.

3. High above me, the giant trees swayed.

4. The waves lashed against the jagged rocks.

5. The light faded and the cold night drew in.

Sometimes more than one adjective may be placed before a noun to give it extra meaning:

a **cool**, **tasty** cocktail   or   a **smooth**, **delicious** milkshake

In these examples, a comma is used to separate the two adjectives, although the word 'and' will do just as well.

Exercise 2.5 ✏

Adjectives can make sentences more interesting by giving more information about places, persons or things. Adjectives have been taken away from the following sentences. Think of some to fill in the gaps.

1. For our holiday this year we visited a _____ island in the Pacific.

2. Beyond the _____ and _____ sand the _____ ocean stretched to the horizon.

3. In the evenings we sat at the bar, sipping _____ cocktails and eating _____ seafood.

4. I took off my sandals and tiptoed into the _____, _____ water.

5. Overhead, the _____ seagulls circled.

Types of sentence
There are four main types of sentence:

A **question** which asks something:
May I have a drink, please?

A **statement** which gives us information:
The aeroplane landed on the island.

An **exclamation** which shows someone's strong feelings about something:
What a baking hot day!

A **command** which tells us to do something:
Fasten your safety belts.

Exercise 2.6

Label each of the following sentences. Write each one and then name the type of sentence it is in brackets. Look carefully at the example first.

Example: Are you sure you would like to go swimming this morning? (question)

1. This is paradise!

2. For room service, dial '0'.

3. The scuba diving course commences at 10.00 am.

4. When would you like breakfast?

5. Keep all belongings with you at all times.

Exercise 2.7

Write **three** sentences of your own for **each** sentence type, making twelve in total. Remember the four types: questions, statements, exclamations and commands.

Can you spell?
Similar letters, different sounds
Some words may look very similar, but they are pronounced differently. Look at the following examples of words which all share the same letter patterns at the end:

tr**ough**   thr**ough**   pl**ough**

They certainly look similar, but the sounds they make are very different.

Exercise 2.8

Match up the following words (1-5) with the words with which they rhyme (a-e):

1. dough   (a) puff

2. bough   (b) no

3. tough   (c) rebuff

4. enough   (d) now

5. through   (e) new

Exercise 2.9

In the following groups of words, the key word can be matched to **one** of the words opposite it. Write each key word and all the group words next to it. Then **underline** the word which is pronounced the **same** as (or rhymes with) the key word.

The first is done for you as an example.

Key Word	Group words
so	to <u>no</u> do
1. most	cost lost host
2. plough	trough bough through
3. now	tow cow low
4. grown	clown town sown
5. come	home some chrome
6. hour	tour sour your
7. tomb	comb womb bomb
8. weight	height eight sleight

Speaking and listening

1. News conference: Imagine you are Michael from *Kensuke's Kingdom*. When you are finally rescued from the desert island you are invited to attend a press conference. Newspaper reporters ask you lots of questions about your extraordinary adventure. In groups of about four, act out this press conference, with one of you playing the part of Michael and the others acting as reporters.

2. Discussion: Imagine you are about to be left alone on a desert island, like Michael in the story. You are allowed three luxuries to take with you to the island. What will you take with you, and why? Take turns to share your thoughts in discussion groups or pairs.

3. Presentations: Find out more about the beautiful islands in the South Pacific where people may take luxury holidays. Working with a partner, choose one particular island, or group of small islands, and give a short presentation to your class. You could talk about the size, location, landscape, facilities, local language and cuisine.

4. Talking pairs: With a partner, perform a short role-play. One of you is really keen to visit the Fijian holiday resort of the Wakaya Club. One of you believes it would be the holiday of a lifetime. Your friend is worried that such a holiday might be too quiet and boring. Working in role, try to persuade your friend that the Wakaya Club is the place to be. Then exchange roles and perform the role-play again.

Have you read?

These are stories and non-fiction books about
sea voyages and other exciting adventures.

Robinson Crusoe (Young Reading) by Daniel Defoe
(Usborne Publishing Ltd)
The Adventurous Four: Shipwrecked! by Enid Blyton
(Collins)
The Adventures of Tintin at Sea by Michael Farr
(John Murray)
The Dolphin Crossing by Jill Paton Walsh (Puffin Books)
*Treasure Island: From the Story by Robert Louis Stevenson (Young Reading Series
Two)* by Angela Wilkes (Usborne Publishing Ltd)
Alone on the Wide Wide Sea by Michael Morpurgo (HarperCollins)
Intrepid Voyagers: Stories of the World's most Adventurous Sailors by Tom Lochhaas
(McGraw-Hill Publishing Co.)
Sailing Solo: The Legendary Sailors and the Great Races by Ellen MacArthur and
Nic Compton (Mitchell Beazley)
Race Against Time by Ellen MacArthur (Michael Joseph Ltd)

Other things to do...

- Find out more about the Fijian Islands. Use encyclopaedias, atlases,
  holiday brochures or Internet websites. Then design your own page
  for a holiday brochure in which you advertise an imaginary hotel you
  have created on one of the islands. Give the hotel luxurious facilities
  and beautiful views.

- Draw a map of an imaginary island. Add some interesting features, like
  a lagoon, some beaches, a tropical forest and perhaps even a smugglers'
  cove. Think of some interesting names for the features of your island.
  Work as neatly as you can so that your map looks like the real thing.

Chapter 3

Inside the giant peach

James discovers a hole in the side of the giant peach, and bravely enters...

Old-green-grasshopper: Look who's here!

Centipede: We've been waiting for you!

James: Oh no! No! [*James acts scared to death and frozen with fear as the curtain opens slowly to reveal Old-green-grasshopper, Spider, Ladybird, Centipede,*
5   *and Earthworm sitting comfortably. Silkworm is curled up asleep in a corner*]

Spider: I'm hungry!

Old-green-grasshopper: I'm famished!

Ladybird: So am I!

Centipede: Everyone's famished! We need food!

10 [*Pause, as all look at James*]

Spider: [*Leaning toward James*] Aren't you hungry?

[*James is still petrified with fear*]

Old-green-grasshopper: [*To James*] What's the matter with you? You look positively ill!

15 **Centipede**: He looks as though he's going to faint any second.

Ladybird: Oh, my goodness, the poor thing! I do believe he thinks it's *him* we are wanting to eat!

[*Everyone roars with laughter*]

All: Oh dear, oh dear! What an awful thought!

20 **Ladybird**: You mustn't be frightened. We wouldn't *dream* of hurting you. You are one of us now, didn't you know that? You are one of the crew. We're all in the same boat.

Old-green-grasshopper: We've been waiting for you all day long. We thought you were never going to turn up. I'm glad you made it.

25 **Centipede**: So, cheer up, my boy, cheer up! And meanwhile I wish you'd come over here and give me a hand with these boots. It takes me hours to get them all off by myself.

[*James crosses the room and kneels beside Centipede*]

Thank you so much. You are very kind.

30 **James**: Well… uh… you have a lot of boots.

Centipede: I have a lot of legs and a lot of feet. One hundred, to
35 be exact. [*Proudly*] I *am* a centipede, you know.

Earthworm: *There* he goes
40 again! He simply cannot stop telling lies about his legs! He's only got forty-two! The
45 trouble is that most people don't bother to count them. And anyway, there is nothing
50 *marvellous*, you know, Centipede, about having a lot of legs.

Centipede: Poor Earthworm. [*Whispering in James's ear*] He's blind, you
55 know. He can't see how splendid I look.

Earthworm: In my opinion, the *really* marvellous thing is to have no legs at all and to be able to walk just the same.

Centipede: You call that *walking*! You're a *slitherer*, that's all you are! You just *slither* along.

60 **Earthworm**: I *glide*.

Centipede: You are a slimy beast.

Earthworm: I am *not* a slimy beast. I am a useful and much-loved creature. Ask any gardener you like. And as for you ...

Centipede: I am a pest! [*Grinning proudly and looking round the room for* 65 *approval*]

Ladybird: He is *so* proud of that, though for the life of me I cannot understand why. Oh... please excuse me... my name is Ladybird.

(From Roald Dahl's James and the Giant Peach, dramatised by Richard George, 1982)

· ·

Exercise 3.1 ✏

Read the passage from *James and the Giant Peach* and then answer the following questions in complete sentences.

1. How can you tell that the creatures inside the peach were expecting James?

2. Why is James 'frozen with fear' when he first climbs into the peach?

3. Why would it take the centipede so long to take off his boots?

4. If you had to sum up Centipede's character in one word, what would it be? Think about how he behaves and how he speaks to the others in the peach.

5. Why do you think Earthworm prefers to think of himself as a glider rather than a slitherer? What is the difference between slithering and gliding?

6. Use a dictionary to find the meanings of the following words:
   (a) *famished* (line 7); (b) *petrified* (line 12); (c) *proudly* (line 35); (d) *slither* (line 59).

Lots of legs

Although you might think so, centipedes do not have a hundred legs, nor do millipedes have a thousand legs. They are not what you expect at all because they are not even insects – they are arthropods, which means they belong to the class of Myriapods which includes spiders and crabs.

5 Centipedes can have between 30 and 346 limbs and they use them for running swiftly and capturing their prey of insects, slugs and earthworms which they usually hunt at night. Most species like to live in warmer climates but many can be found in cooler places such as Britain.

Centipede

10 Millipedes are not hunters but are much gentler creatures. They eat dead plants, so they like to live in moist piles of decaying leaves and this helps them to keep their temperature constant. They usually have between 80 and 400 limbs but the Californian millipede

15 *Illacme plenipes* has the most of any arthropod – 750!

Centipede facts:

The Amazonian giant centipede can be up to 30 cm long and will eat bats as well as small rodents and insects.

20 The young centipede usually hatches with 7 pairs of legs and grows more each time it moults.

Millipede

Millipede facts:

Millipedes are powerful burrowers, using their legs and body in a wave-
25 like motion to force their way underground.

They protect themselves from predators by coiling tightly, keeping their hard exoskeleton exposed.

Some millipedes can emit a poisonous liquid which can irritate the skin and eyes of larger predators.

Exercise 3.2 ✏

Read the passage about centipedes and millipedes, then use complete sentences to answer the following questions:

1. What is meant by the term *myriapods*?

2. Do all centipedes have a hundred legs as their name suggests? Explain as fully as you can.

3. In what ways are millipedes more gentle than centipedes?

4. Where do millipedes like to live?

5. How do millipedes protect themselves from predators?

6. Use a dictionary to help you find the meanings of the following words:
   (a) *arthropods* (line 3); (b) *species* (line 7); (c) *rodents* (line 19);
   (d) *exoskeleton* (line 27).

. . . .

Exercise 3.3 ✏

Your turn to write:

1. Read the passage from *James and the Giant Peach* again. Continue the play in your own words. What do you think might happen next?

2. Put yourself in James's shoes as he enters the peach for the first time. How do you feel? Write your thoughts in a few sentences. Do you think you are going to be dinner for the insects?

3. Draw diagrams of a centipede and a millipede and then write labels and captions to accompany them. Try to give as much information as you can about each one.

4. Find out more about the class of animals called *myriapods*. Then write the information you have found in a factfile of your own.

Learning about language

Verbs

In the first passage Centipede accuses Earthworm of **slithering**. But Earthworm prefers to think of himself as **gliding** along instead, which he thinks sounds much better.

Slither and **glide** are **verbs**, or 'doing words'. They tell us what the subject of a sentence is doing – in this case that Earthworm is moving.

Look at these examples of verbs in action:

James **crept** inside the peach.

Ladybird **smiled** at James.

The insects **laughed** out loud.

Exercise 3.4 ✏

Copy the following sentences and underline the verb(s).

1. James thought the insects might hurt him.

2. Centipede grinned proudly.

3. Everyone roared with laughter.

4. Centipedes eat soft-bodied insects.

5. Millipedes live in damp places.

If something is **gliding** we think of it as shiny and proud. But something which slithers seems sneaky, dirty or even slimy. So verbs not only tell us what something is **doing**. They can sometimes tell us what it **looks like** and how it **behaves** while doing it. Look at these examples:

The man **walked** down the road
The man **hobbled** down the road.

The princess **walked** into the ballroom.
The princess **glided** into the ballroom.

In these examples, the second sentence of each pair tells us much more about what is going on.

. . . .

Exercise 3.5

Replace the verbs underlined with more interesting ones, to create a clearer picture of what is happening.

1. The football player <u>ran</u> towards the ball.

2. The dancer <u>moved</u> across the dance floor.

3. The rain <u>fell</u> onto the school roof.

4. 'I feel so happy!' James <u>said</u>.

5. The little mouse <u>went</u> into a corner and hid.

. . . .

Exclamation marks

Read the passage from *James and the Giant Peach* once again and see how many exclamation marks (!) you can find.

You will see there are lots. Exclamation marks are used to mark sudden, unexpected remarks.

Exclamation marks are often used to show:

- **surprise**   Gosh! I wasn't expecting that!

- **pleasure**   What a beautiful present! Thank you!

- **anger**   Andrew! Take your foot off your brother's head!

- **fear**   Oh no! They're going to gobble me up!

- **humour**   ... and then his head fell off!

Richard George, who wrote the play version of Roald Dahl's *James and the Giant Peach*, likes to use exclamation marks a lot. In a play, exclamation marks can be especially useful because they instruct an actor to speak a sentence loudly and with expression. But beware: if you use too many exclamation marks they lose their effect so your writing has less impact.

Exercise 3.6 ✏

The following passage once contained lots of exclamation marks, but they have been replaced with full stops and commas. Where do you think they should be? Rewrite the passage putting some exclamation marks back in place. But not too many!

Joseph and his father were spending the day at the fair.

'I don't want to go in,' exclaimed Joseph. 'It's too dark inside.'

'Don't be silly,' said his father. 'It's only pretend. It's not a real ghost train.'

'But I'm frightened,' said his son.

'You'll be fine. Just hold my hand.' said Dad.

They climbed into a carriage and soon disappeared into the darkness.

'Wow,' said Joseph. 'It's amazing.'

'Help,' cried Dad. 'Stop the train. I want to get off.'

'But I thought you said it's only pretend,' said Joseph. 'Who's the Daddy now?'

Exercise 3.7 ✏

Which of the following sentences do you think require an exclamation mark? Write each one, putting an exclamation mark only when you think it is needed.

1. What an amazing picture.

2. We ate our dinner in the garden.

3. I'm not going up there; it's too high.

4. Sit down at once.

5. Mary will be arriving at ten o'clock.

Can you spell?
Common endings: –able / –ible

Many words end in either **–able** or **–ible**. The problem is that because they sound so similar, it is difficult to know which one is used when.

Look at these examples:

vegetable   terrible

reasonable   visible

Do you think the endings (or 'suffixes') for these words sound similar?

There is no easy way to remember when to use which ending. So the best way is just to memorise what they look like so that you will notice when you spell them incorrectly. For example, 'terrable' looks wrong doesn't it? In fact, it looks terrible!

. . . .

Exercise 3.8

Write a sentence containing each of the following words. Remember to spell them correctly as they are here.

1. horrible
2. miserable
3. sensible
4. table
5. reasonable

Exercise 3.9

Write the following sentences and fill in the missing letter correctly. You may need to use a dictionary or spell-checker to help you.

1. The space crew said that an early launch was imposs_ble.

2. He packed his port_ble radio in his suitcase.

3. The winning carrot was an incred_ble size.

4. Passengers are respons_ble for their own luggage.

5. She had so much prep to do that it was quite unmanage_ble.

6. The force field around the alien ship was invisi_ble.

7. The centre forward's attempts to score had been absolutely laugh_ble.

8. The doughnut, bursting with jam, looked irresist_ble.

Speaking and listening

1. Divide into groups of about three or four. Then read the passage from *James and the Giant Peach* together, taking a character each and doubling up if you need to. As you read the script aloud, take special notice of the exclamation marks, and use lots of expression whenever you see one.

2. Which insects do you like? Perhaps you don't like any? If you had to choose a favourite, what would it be? Sit in a circle and take turns talking for a minute about your own favourite insects.

3. If 'creepy crawlies' could speak our language, how might they sound? What sort of voices would they have? Would a grasshopper sound wise, or a wasp speak very quickly? Would an earthworm drone on in a slow laborious voice? In small groups, take on the roles of some talking creatures.

4. Working with a partner, write, rehearse and perform a short sketch between a centipede and a millipede, each one believing that he or she belongs to the better species.

Have you read?

The following books are packed with interesting information, pictures and diagrams of the 'creepy crawlies' around us.

Bugs and Minibeasts (The Illustrated Wildlife Encyclopedia) by John Farndon (Southwater)
Insects (Collins Gem Series) by Michael Chinery (Southwater)
Minibeasts (Knowledge Masters Series) by Neil Morris (Belitha Press Ltd)
1001 Bugs to Spot by G. Doherty (Usborne Publishing Ltd)
Insects (What's inside? DK Paperback) by Dorling Kindersley Publishing (Dorling Kindersley Publishing)
Insects and other Minibeasts by Barbara Taylor (Oxford University Press)

Gerald Durrell was fascinated by insects (and other animals) from an early age. He wrote about his amazing discoveries in
his many stories, which include:

My Family and Other Animals (Puffin Books)
A Zoo in My Luggage (Penguin Books Ltd)
Birds, Beasts and Relatives (Penguin Books Ltd)
Encounters with Animals (Penguin Books Ltd)
Menagerie Manor (House of Stratus)

Other things to do...

- Find a copy of Richard George's play version of Roald Dahl's *James and the Giant Peach*. Then perform scenes from it together in class. You might even be able to perform the play in assembly, or as a school play.

- Find out more about the fascinating world of insects by visiting the following websites: www.easyinsects.co.uk
www.nhm.ac.uk/nature-online/life/insects-spiders

- The next time you are in your garden at home, or the playground at school, get down onto the ground and spend a few moments looking at the thousands (or even millions) of insects that share our gardens with us. You'll be surprised at what you might find. Insects lived on Earth millions of years before Man and probably they will be here well after we have gone.

Chapter 4

A surprising find

Jessica and her friends are exploring the cliffs and caves where the river meets the sea at Clademouth. They know they shouldn't have come this far alone, and are just about to head back, when they make a very unusual discovery…

'Look,' said Jessica, 'I think we ought to go back. We'll get into awful trouble if anything happens to Tim.'

'That's just an excuse,' said Tim. 'You're just frightened like the rest of us.'

5   'All right, I am frightened,' said Jessica. 'All this earth slid about during the night, and who's to say it won't go on sliding about and trap us underneath it. This whole lot could shift at any minute. It's too dangerous here.'

And shift it did. As Jessica spoke, the ground they sat on rippled and flexed, and the slope they had slid down reared up and twisted. The
10 slope was a neck. Fergus ran the light of the torch up it, and found a small pointed head. As the terrified children watched, two yellow eyes opened and blinked. Fergus dropped the torch which must never be moved from the shelf inside the kitchen door, and the children ran towards the light, stumbling over each other and gasping for breath, their lungs tight with
15 fear. They tumbled out on to the ruins of the cliff, and lay panting in the morning sun. None of them spoke.

But something did. From deep in the cavern, with a strange sound like the wind over milk bottles (which the children had never heard, for milk bottles had not been used for years) they heard something singing. It
20 sang one word, over and over again.

'Frightened. Frightened. Frightened.'

'I'm going to see what it is,' said Jessica. 'The rest of you stay here.'

'Rubbish! We're all going with you,' said Billy.

'Besides,' said Tim, 'we've got to get the torch back.'

25 It took some time for their eyes to re-adjust to the gloom. It took a little more time to realize what it was they were looking at, for the dinosaur nearly filled the cavern, and they could not see right to the far end of her. But the two browny-grey tree trunk legs and the long neck with its pointed, duck-like head (and still those yellow eyes blinking worriedly at
30 them) left them with only one possible conclusion.

'It's a dinosaur.' said Dixie.

(From Brilliant the Dinosaur by Richard Stilgoe, 1994)

Exercise 4.1 ✏

Read the passage from Richard Stilgoe's *Brilliant the Dinosaur* and then answer the following questions in complete sentences.

1. How many children were exploring the caves together? Can you name them all?

2. Why was Jessica frightened?

3. What happened to the ground as Jessica was speaking?

4. The children left something behind as they ran out of the cavern - what was it?

5. What do you think the phrase 'their lungs tight with fear' (line 14) means?

6. Find dictionary definitions of the following words: (a) *reared* (line 9); (b) *ruins* (line 15); (c) *cavern* (line 17); (d) *conclusion* (line 30).

· ·

The long-necked beast

The Diplodocus was one of the biggest dinosaurs ever to walk the Earth. It belonged to a group of dinosaurs called *sauropods*. It was 26m long and its great weight (15 tons) was supported by huge straight legs, like pillars.

5 The Diplodocus looked extraordinary with its long neck and tail, and a head that was tiny in proportion to the rest of its body. This type of body suited its lifestyle perfectly. It could reach up to feed at the tops of the very tall trees, like conifers, that grew at the time. Its small head allowed it to browse amongst the vegetation, where few other dinosaurs could reach.

10 This type of feeding needed a special type of neck – one that was strong, light, and flexible, in order to be raised and lowered easily. Having stripped one area bare of food, it would have ambled off with its companions in search of new feeding grounds. If Diplodocus was threatened by a meat eater, its only defence would have been its bulk, and its long, whip-like tail.

15 Although Diplodocus is often shown living in marshy land, this habitat would not have suited it at all. Because it had quite narrow feet in

proportion to its body weight (like an elephant's), it probably would have sunk into the mire
20 and got stuck. It would have preferred a landscape with dry, firm ground, where it would browse its way through conifer forests, perhaps as part of a
25 herd.

The design of a Diplodocus's neck is rather like that of a man-made crane. The jib, which juts out from the main tower and from which the hooks used for lifting are
30 suspended, is like the dinosaur's neck. The heavy base of the crane which keeps it from toppling over is like a Diplodocus's sturdy body. The jib of a crane has to be light and strong, so the engineer builds it with a light metal framework. Diplodocus had lightweight, but very strong, bones in its neck, which it could raise and lower like the jib of a crane.

(From Eyewitness Guides: Dinosaur by David Norman and Angela Milner, 1989)

Exercise 4.2 ✏

Read the passage entitled 'The long-necked beast' and then answer the following questions in complete sentences.

1. The Diplodocus belongs to which group of dinosaurs?

2. In what ways was the dinosaur's body well suited to its lifestyle?

3. If the Diplodocus had been attacked, how might it have defended itself?

4. Why would the Diplodocus have preferred a dry landscape to a marshy one?

5. In what ways was a Diplodocus like a man-made crane?

6. Write the meanings of the following words. You may use a dictionary to help you: (a) *pillars* (line 4); (b) *vegetation* (line 9); (c) *ambled* (line 12); (d) *habitat* (line 15); (e) *mire* (line 19).

Exercise 4.3 ✏

Your turn to write:

1. Imagine you are one of the children in the excerpt from *Brilliant the Dinosaur*. You have been exploring the cliffs with your friends when you discover the ancient creature. You think it must be a dinosaur, but you can't quite believe your eyes. Write a paragraph describing what you see and how you feel.

2. What do you know about dinosaurs? In the story, we learn that Tim has done a project on dinosaurs. What might you find in such a project? Put together a mini-project in which you write what you know (or can find out) about one or more dinosaurs. Include labelled diagrams and sketches.

3. Imagine you are the curator (manager) of a new dinosaur museum about to open in a major city. You need to advertise the museum so that residents and visitors to the city will know about it. Design and produce a leaflet that gives people information about the museum in a persuasive way. Remember to include important details, such as opening times, ticket prices and location.

4. Write a story in which you make a surprising discovery of a new kind of dinosaur skeleton, of a type never before seen. Perhaps palaeontologists (fossil experts) might name the dinosaur after you. Think of an interesting setting for your story.

5. Write an acrostic poem about a Diplodocus. Remember, in an acrostic poem, the first letter of each line can be read vertically to form a special word – in this case, **DIPLODOCUS**.

- -

Learning about language
Missing letters
Sometimes, especially when we are speaking, we shorten words and join others together by missing out letters. For example, we might say,

'**We'll** go with you.' instead of '**We will** go with you.'

Here, we have missed out the letters 'w' and 'i' from the word 'will'. It is shorter and easier for us to say. The shortened version is called a **contraction** and an **apostrophe** (') is needed in place of the missing letter or letters.

Look at the following examples of contractions in which an apostrophe has been used to show where the missing letters would have been.

I have   becomes   **I've**   (the missing letters are: *h* and *a*)

You will   becomes   **you'll**   (the missing letters are: *w* and *i*)

Exercise 4.4 🖉

Copy and complete the following table of contractions.

Full version	Contraction	Missing letters
	I'll	w, i
I would	I'd	
I cannot		n, o
	you've	
he has		

Exercise 4.5 🖉

In the extract from *Brilliant the Dinosaur* the children often use contractions when they speak. Identify the proper words for each contraction they have used. Write each sentence, replacing the underlined contraction with its full version.

1. 'We'll get into awful trouble if anything happens to Tim.'

2. 'That's just an excuse,' said Tim.

3. 'You're just frightened like the rest of us.'

4. 'I'm going to see what it is,' said Jessica.'

5. 'We're all going with you,' said Billy.

6. 'We've got to get the torch back.'

Notice how all the questions in Exercise 4.5 involve speech. Contractions often appear in story speech as authors like to make their characters' conversations seem real. (Most of us use contractions in our conversations every day.)

It is better to avoid using contractions in formal writing, such as letters, essays and examination questions.

. . . .

Its and it's

Look at the following sentences, taken from the second passage:

The Diplodocus looked extraordinary with its long neck and tail, and a head that was tiny in proportion to the rest of its body. This type of body suited its lifestyle perfectly.

Can you see the word **its** being used? How many times does it appear? There is no apostrophe needed here because the word **its** has no missing letters. It does not mean 'it is' or 'it has'.

Now look at the following sentence which you will recognise from the first passage:

It's too dangerous here.

In this example, the word **it's** is a contraction and is two words 'contracted' together: **It is** becomes **It's**. An apostrophe is needed to show that the letter 'i' has been missed out, like the examples in Exercise 4.4.

The rule is that you need an apostrophe in **it's** only when it means 'it is' or 'it has'. At all other times use **its**.

Exercise 4.6 ✏️

Copy the following sentences, filling each space with **either** the word *its* **or** the contraction *it's*.

1. The dinosaur reached high into the trees to find _____ dinner.

2. 'We had better run! I think _____ starting to rain!' said Tim.

3. We don't know whether _____ a bone from a Diplodocus or a Mamenchisaurus.

4. The Diplodocus thundered _____ way down to the lakeside.

5. The dinosaur museum opened _____ doors to the public at ten o'clock.

6. '_____ five-thirty and we still haven't seen the T-Rex!' said the visitor.

. . . .

Can you spell?
Big, bigger, biggest

Read the following few lines:

The giraffes we see today have very long necks. The neck of a Diplodocus was even longer, but the longest neck of all belonged to a Mamenchisaurus and was 10m long.

In these sentences the words **long**, **longer** and **longest** are used to show the size of the animals' necks compared with other, larger, ones. It is difficult for us to understand how large or small something is unless we can **compare** it with something else. So we use **comparative** and **superlative** adjectives to help us.

For many comparative adjectives you simply add **–er** and for superlatives you add **–est** without changing the spelling:

adjective	comparative	superlative
tall	tall**er**	tall**est**

Exercise 4.7 ✏

Write these adjectives and add the appropriate comparative and superlative endings:

1. damp   **4.** round

2. new   **5.** bold

3. neat

Other comparatives and superlatives need more spelling changes before a new ending can be added. For example:

For the word 'lazy' change the **y** to **i** to make: laz**y**, laz**i**er, laz**i**est.

Repeat the last letter of 'thin' to make: thi**n**, thi**nn**er, thi**nn**est.

The word nice already ends in **–e**, so you add **–r** and **–st** to make: nic**e**, nic**er**, nic**est**.

· ·

Exercise 4.8 ✏

Copy the following table of comparative and superlative adjectives and fill in the gaps. Be careful to think about the spelling changes that you may have to make. The first set has been done for you.

cold	colder	coldest
wide		
	prettier	
		loveliest
slim		
	braver	
		closest

Speaking and listening

1. In groups of five, act the scene from the passage in which the children explore the cliffs by the sea at Clademouth and make the astonishing discovery. Rehearse your scene and then perform it to the rest of the class.

2. Word tennis: Research the different names of dinosaurs and then, in pairs, take turns to name a dinosaur. Each time you 'serve' with a name your playing partner has to 'return' with another name. Keep playing until someone 'drops the ball' (i.e. runs out of dinosaurs, or hesitates).

3. Choose a particular dinosaur and prepare a two minute talk on it. Then present it to the rest of the class. Try to make use of pictures and diagrams in your talk too: audiences generally like something to look at as well as listen to. You will need to think about the dinosaur's name, habitat, diet, size and weight.

4. Hot-seating: In groups of five or six, form a circle around a chair (the 'hot seat'). Take turns to sit in the hot seat, taking on the role of one of the children in the passage. The others in the group may ask you questions about what you saw and how you felt when you discovered the dinosaur in the cave at Clademouth.

· ·

Have you read?

If you like reading stories with dinosaurs in them, then try the following books:

Dinosaur in Danger by Paul Geraghty (Red Fox)
Saturday Night at the Dinosaur Stomp by Carol Diggory Shields (Walker Books Ltd)
Dinosaur Stories (Kingfisher Treasury of Stories) by Jeremy Strong (Kingfisher)
The Mystery of the Dinosaur Bones by David A. Adler (Puffin Books)
Jurassic Park by Michael Crichton (Pocket)

The Lost World by Michael Crichton (Arrow)
The Village Dinosaur by Phyllis Arkle (Puffin)

Read these non-fiction books and become an expert on dinosaurs (or a palaeontologist, as they are called).

Encyclopedia Prehistorica Dinosaurs: The Definitive Popup by Robert Clarke Sabuda (Candlewick Press)
The Complete Guide to Prehistoric Life by Tim Haines (BBC Books)
Walking with Dinosaurs: A Natural History by Tim Haines (BBC Books)
First Encyclopedias of Dinosaurs and Prehistoric Life (First Encyclopedias) by Sam Taplin
The Best Ever Book of Dinosaurs by Michael Benton (Kingfisher Books Ltd)
The DK Big Book of Dinosaurs by Angela Wilkes (Dorling Kindersley)

Other things to do...

- How many other words can you make from the word Diplodocus? You could start with slip, plod and soil. Try to do the same with other dinosaur names, for example: Stegosaurus, Brontosaurus, Mamenchisaurus, Tyrannosaurus.

- Compile an 'amazing factfile' on dinosaurs, in which you list some interesting facts such as the heaviest, the tallest, the longest, the earliest and the latest dinosaurs. You may be able to display your findings as a special feature in the school magazine, or on a wall display in school. You will need to do some research first.

- Bring in any videos and CD ROMs you may have at home on the subject of dinosaurs. Compile and discuss the resources you have in class. You could share your items together during a special 'Dino Day'.

Chapter 5

The Railway Children

When their father is wrongfully accused of being a spy and sent to prison, Roberta, Peter and Phyllis are forced to move to rural Yorkshire with their mother. In the quiet countryside they have only the sound of the passing trains to remind them of the life they once enjoyed in the city.

After the adventure of Peter's coal-mine, it seemed well to the children to keep away from the station – but they did not, they could not, keep away from the railway. They had lived all their lives in a street where cabs and omnibuses rumbled by at all hours, and the carts of butchers and bakers
5   and candlestick makers (I never saw a candlestick maker's cart; did you?) might occur at any moment. Here in the deep silence of the sleeping country the only things that went by were the trains. They seemed to be all that was left to link the children to the old life that had once been theirs.

10   Straight down the hill in front of Three Chimneys the daily passage of their six feet began to mark a path across the crisp, short turf. They began to know the hours when certain trains passed, and they gave names to them. The 9.15 up was called the Green Dragon. The 10.7 down was the Worm of Wantley. The midnight town express, whose shrieking rush
15   they sometimes woke from their dreams to hear, was the Fearsome Fly-by-night. Peter got up once, in chill starshine, and, peeping at it through his curtain named it on the spot.

It was by the Green Dragon that the old gentleman travelled. He was a very nice-looking old gentleman, and he looked as if he were nice, too,
20   which is not at all the same thing. He had a fresh-coloured, clean-shaven face and white hair, and he wore rather odd-shaped collars and a top-hat that wasn't exactly the same kind as other people's. Of course the children didn't see all this at first. In fact the first thing they noticed about the old gentleman was his hand.

25   It was one morning as they sat on the fence waiting for the Green Dragon, which was three and a quarter minutes late by Peter's Waterbury watch that he had had given him on his last birthday.

'The Green Dragon's going where Father is,' said Phyllis; 'if it were a really real dragon, we could stop it and ask it to take our love to Father.'

30 'Dragons don't carry people's love,' said Peter, 'they'd be above it.'

'Yes, they do, if you tame them thoroughly first. They fetch and carry like spaniels,' said Phyllis, 'and feed out of your hand. I wonder why Father never writes to us.'

'Mother says he's been too busy,' said Bobbie; 'but he'll write soon she
35 says.'

'I say,' Phyllis suggested, 'let's all wave to the Green Dragon as
40 it goes by. If it's a magic dragon, it'll understand and take our love to Father. And if it
45 isn't, three waves aren't much. We shall never miss them.'

So when the
50 Green Dragon tore shrieking out of the mouth of its dark lair,

which was the tunnel, all three children stood on the railing and waved
55 their pocket-handkerchiefs without stopping to think whether they were clean handkerchiefs or the reverse. They were, as a matter of fact, very much the reverse.

And out of a first-class carriage a hand waved back. A quite clean hand. It held a newspaper. It was the old gentleman's hand.

60 After this it became the custom for waves to be exchanged between the children and the 9.15.

And the children, especially the girls, liked to think that perhaps the old gentleman knew Father, and would meet him 'in business', wherever that shady retreat might be, and tell him how his three children stood on a rail
65 far away in the green country and waved their love to him every morning, wet or fine.

(From The Railway Children by E. Nesbit, first published in 1906)

- -

Exercise 5.1 ✏

Read the passage from *The Railway Children* and then answer the following questions in complete sentences.

1. Why were the children so keen to visit the railway? What did they find so appealing about the passing trains?

2. The children gave the trains different names as they passed each day. Write the three names mentioned in the passage.

3. Describe the old gentleman's appearance.

4. What was the first thing the children noticed about the old gentleman?

5. What is the reason given to the children for Father not writing to them?

6. Why are the children waving to the 9.15? What are they hoping to achieve?

7. Use a dictionary to find the meanings of the following words:
   (a) *omnibuses* (line 4); (b) *tame* (line 31); (c) *lair* (line 53); (d) *custom* (line 60); (e) *retreat* (line 64).

Steaming ahead

Horses, oxen or people provided the pulling power for cars on rails and roads for thousands of years. In the 1800s, inventors came up with an alternative. They worked out how to use steam power for pulling wheeled vehicles. In 1825, the world's first public steam railway, the
5 25-mile long Stockton and Darlington line, opened in England. On its

opening day, the train hauled both freight and passenger cars. Later, it was used mainly for carrying coal. Five years later, the Liverpool and Manchester line opened with its new, steam-driven passenger trains. The company had run a competition called the Rainhill Trials to find the best
10 locomotive for its railway. Both horse-drawn and steam locomotives took part. The steam-driven *Rocket* won.

The success of the *Rocket* convinced investors to back the development of steam-powered locomotives. The brains behind the *Rocket* and the Stockton and Darlington and Liverpool and Manchester railways were
15 George Stephenson and his son Robert. In 1823, they set up the world's first locomotive factory. Other British engineers began to experiment with steam power, and locomotives were made for use in Britain and around the world.

Great Moments on the Railways

20 | 1769 | Frenchman Nicolas Cugnot builds the first steam-powered vehicle.

1804 | British Engineer Richard Trevithick tests the first steam locomotive for the Penydarran Ironworks in Wales.

1825 | The Stockton and Darlington Railway opens in
25 | Britain – the first public railroad to use steam-powered locomotives.

1829 | Robert and George Stephenson's Rocket wins the Rainhill Trials. It becomes the locomotive used for the Liverpool and Manchester Railway.

30 | 1840s | Semaphore Signalling is introduced. The first tickets for train journeys are issued.

1863 | London Underground's Metropolitan Line opens and is the world's first underground passenger railroad.

1883 | The Luxurious Orient Express first runs on June 5 from
35 | Paris, France, to Bucharest in Romania.

1893 | The New York Central and Hudson River Railroad claims that its steam locomotive No. 999 travels faster than 100mph.

1900 | The Paris Metro opens.

40 | 1904 | The New York City Subway opens.

1938 | Mallard sets the world speed record for a steam-powered locomotive (126mph)

1955 | The world's most powerful single-unit diesel-electric locomotives, the Deltics, first run between London and
45 | Liverpool.

1980 | The first electromagnetic trains (Maglevs) open at Birmingham Airport in Britain.

1981	TGV (Train a Grande Vitesse) first runs between Paris and Lyon in France.
50 1994	Channel Tunnel completed, linking rail networks in Britain and the Continent.
1996	Maglev Train on the Yamanashi test line in Japan reaches a staggering 350mph.

(From All About Trains, edited by Michael Harris, 2004)

Exercise 5.2

Read the passage about trains and then answer the following questions in complete sentences.

1. (a) What was the name of the world's first public steam railway?

   (b) How long was it?

2. Which competition did George Stephenson win?

3. Where and when did the world's first underground passenger railroad open?

4. Where did the Orient Express travel to and from during its maiden journey?

5. (a) What are 'Maglevs'?

   (b) What are 'Deltics'?

6. How many years after the London Underground opened did a similar subway first appear in New York?

7. Use a dictionary to help you find meanings of the following words:
   (a) *hauled* (line 6); (b) *freight* (line 6); (c) *investors* (line 12);
   (d) *subway* (line 40); (e) *networks* (line 50).

Exercise 5.3

Your turn to write:

1. Re-read the passage from *The Railway Children*. Then continue the story in your own words. What do you think might happen next? Will the children meet the old gentleman? Will he offer them his help?

2. Write about a time when you have enjoyed a train journey. Think about:

   • where you travelled to and from

   • the train's appearance

   • the sights and sounds along the journey.

3. Write a poem entitled 'The Green Dragon'. Describe the kind of steam engine that features in the passage, roaring through the countryside, blowing out steam as it passes. Remember to imagine the sights, sounds and smells.

4. Write a paragraph or two as if you were the old gentleman on the train in the first passage. Describe the moment when you first saw the three children waving at the train and how, each morning, you enjoy seeing their smiling faces as you travel to work in the city.

Learning about language
Pronouns (1): Personal pronouns

Pronouns take the place of nouns. They help us to avoid repeating ourselves:

Gran dropped crumbs everywhere as Gran chomped through the chocolate.
*Gran dropped crumbs everywhere as **she** chomped through the chocolate cake.*

Mrs Baker marked Paulo's work and then returned the work
*Mrs Baker marked Paulo's work and then returned **it**.*

In the first example Gran is the **subject** of the verb – it is she who is chomping through the chocolate cake. When the personal pronoun is replacing the subject of the verb it will be one of the following:

Singular	Plural
I	we
you	you
he, she, it	they

In the second example Paulo's work is the **object** of the verb – i.e. Mrs Baker is returning *it*. When the noun being replaced is the object of the verb then we change it to one of the following personal pronouns:

Singular	Plural
me	us
you	you
him, her, it	them

Be sure not to confuse when to use **subject pronouns** (particularly **I** and **we**) and when to use **object pronouns** (particularly **me** and **us**).

Exercise 5.4 🖉

In each of these sentences the words underlined are the subject of the verb. Rewrite each one using personal pronouns to avoid some of the repetition.

1. Mr Halliwell told us that <u>Mr Halliwell</u> had been to Jamaica in the holidays.

2. 'Sally, when will <u>Sally</u> be here?' I asked.

3. The day trip was fun but <u>the day trip</u> was over too quickly!

4. Mum gave me a necklace <u>Mum</u> had bought.

5. The football players boasted that <u>the football players</u> would win the game with ease.

Exercise 5.5 ✏️

In the following sentences the noun to be replaced is the object of the verb. Rewrite each one using personal pronouns.

1. Uncle Tom said we should thank <u>Uncle Tom</u> for the weekend.
2. I wrote to the players to congratulate <u>the players</u> on their glorious win.
3. For Dad's birthday I gave <u>Dad</u> a gold fountain pen.
4. When Mum gets home I shall make <u>Mum</u> a nice cup of tea.
5. The weather started well but we saw <u>the weather</u> become worse as the day wore on.

Study the following sentences:

Sally and I are going shopping tomorrow.

Mrs Baker was teaching Sally and me.

In the first sentence, 'Sally and I' are the subject. In the second sentence, 'Sally and me' are the object.

Exercise 5.6 ✏️

Write out the sentences below using the correct pronoun from those given:

1. Peter and I/me went swimming.
2. Sally and he/him were friends.
3. Did you see we/us yesterday?
4. They heard you and I/me laughing.
5. You and I/me will go home together.

Simple sentences

A **simple sentence** is a single statement consisting of a **subject** and a **verb**. Many sentances also have an **object**. Look at the following example:

The children	saw	the old gentleman	on the train.
subject	**verb**	**object**	

The children are the subject of this simple sentence. They are doing the seeing. The gentleman is the object, because it is he who is being seen. Here is another simple sentence:

George Stephenson	invented	the Rocket steam engine.
subject	**verb**	**object**

Every sentence needs a verb to make it a complete grammatical sentence.

Exercise 5.7 🖉

Write the following simple sentences underlining the verb in each one.

1. The children moved to the countryside.

2. The Green Dragon roared through the countryside.

3. Peter heard the midnight express go by.

4. The gentleman smiled at the children.

5. Phyllis missed her father very much.

Exercise 5.8 🖉

Write these sentences underlining the subject in blue and the object in red.

1. Trains replaced horses and oxen.

2. Inventors discovered steam power.

3. The train hauled passenger cars.

4. The company held a competition.

5. Robert Stephenson assisted his father George.

Remember, simple sentences do not necessarily have an object. For example:

Peter	laughed.	The crowd	gasped.
subject	**verb**	**subject**	**verb**

Exercise 5.9

Write these sentences underlining the subject in blue and the verb in green.

1. Roberta waved and waved.

2. The gentleman smiled back.

3. The Green Dragon trundled on.

4. The London Underground opened in 1863.

5. At last the Channel Tunnel was complete.

Can you spell?
Prefixes and suffixes

Prefixes and **suffixes** are groups of letters that can be added to other words (called roots) to make other words. A **prefix** is added to the beginning of the word:

mis + *understand* = *misunderstand*

multi + *coloured* = *multicoloured*

A **suffix** is added to the end of the word:

friend + **less** = *friendless*   *praise* + **worthy** = *praiseworthy*

Some root words can have both a prefix *and* a suffix added to them.

un + kind + **ness** = unkindness

Exercise 5.10 ✏

Complete the following words by choosing the correct prefix from the words below.

    mis–   semi–   pre–   dis–   un–

1. ___happy

2. ___ordained

3. ___circle

4. ___appoint

5. ___interpret

Exercise 5.11 ✏

Now do the same for the following words, using the suffixes below.

    –ness   –ment   –ship   –ful   –en

1. good___

2. help___

3. strength___

4. content___

5. friend___

Speaking and listening

1. Hot seating: Take turns in class to sit in the 'hot seat' at the front of the room as one of the characters from The Railway Children. Answer questions from your friends. When it is your turn to ask the character some questions, try to think about his or her feelings during the scene in the passage.

2. Do you like travelling on trains? What is your favourite way of getting about? Sailing, flying, driving or even ballooning, perhaps? Give a short speech to the class about your favourite way of travelling. Give some reasons for your choice.

3. Memory Game: Sit in a circle, either as a whole class or in groups. Take turns around the circle to say the following line: 'When I was on a steam train, chugging through the rain, I saw...' When you get to the end of the line, you can add a place, animal or thing that you might see on your journey, but first you must list the items that others have chosen before you so the list gets longer and longer.

4. There are some very famous poems about trains. Many have an interesting rhythm when you read them aloud, like the sound of a real train going by. Look at the following poems, and then practise reading them aloud:

   Night Mail by W. H. Auden

   Song of the Train by David McCord

   Skimbleshanks: The Railway Cat by T.S. Eliot
   From a Railway Carriage by Robert Louis Stevenson

Have you read?

These stories and poems involve train rides and other great journeys.

Mr Majeika and the Ghost Train by Humphrey Carpenter (Puffin Books)
The Train to Glasgow by Wilma Horsbrugh (Clarion Books)
The Railway Phantoms by Dennis Hamley (Back to Front)
Train Song by Diane Siebert (Harper Trophy)
The Railway Cat by Phyllis Arkle (Puffin Books)

Here are some non-fiction books which offer you lots of information on trains.

All About Trains edited by Michael Harris (Southwater)
Trains (First Discovery Series) by James Prunier (Moonlight Publishing Ltd)
Mega Book of Trains by Lynne Gibbs (Chrysalis Children's Books)
Orphan Train Rider: One Boy's True Story by Andrea Warren (Houghton Mifflin)
Trains by Stephanie Turnbull (Usborne Publishing Ltd)

Other things to do...

- Use the Internet, books and magazines to find out more about steam trains. Then put together a short talk, in pairs or on your own, for your class to enjoy.

- Read E. Nesbit's *The Railway Children*. Once you have read some or all of it, watch the film versions too. Then compare the book with the films. Did the plot change? Were the characters as you expected? Was the setting for each film as you had imagined it?

- Write a story that involves a steam engine. Create an interesting setting for your story. Perhaps you could set it in the past, as in *The Railway Children*, when steam trains were common. Your main character might be catching a train for the very first time, perhaps leaving the city for a holiday in the countryside.

Chapter 6

Circus Elephant

Does the Elephant remember
In the grey light before dawn,
Old noises of the jungle
In mornings long gone?
5 Does the Elephant remember
The cry of hungry beasts,
The Tiger and the Leopard,
The Lion at his feasts?
Do his mighty eardrums listen
10 For the thunder of the feet
Of the Buffalo and the Zebra
In the dark and dreadful heat?
Does His Majesty remember,
Does he stir himself and dream
15 Of the long-forgotten music
Of a long-forgotten dream?

Kathryn Worth (From A Trunkful of Elephants edited by Judith Nicholls, 1994)

Wolf

Mine is the howl
that chills the spine
in the forest gloom;
mine is the whine.
5 Mine is the nose
that breathes in fear
when danger's close;
mine is the ear.
Mine is the fur
10 the huntsman trade;
mine is the fur,
I am afraid.

Judith Nicholls (From Dragonsfire by Judith Nicholls, 1990)

Exercise 6.1 ✏️

Read the two poems above and answer the following questions using proper sentences.

1. In Kathryn Worth's poem above, where does the elephant live now?

2. Why do you think the poet refers to the elephant as 'His Majesty' in line 13?

3. Do you think this elephant is a happy one?

4. In the poem 'Wolf' by Judith Nicholls, what do you think the phrase 'chills the spine' might mean in line 2?

5. The word 'mine' is repeated many times in 'Wolf'. What effect do you think this has? Does it make you think about the wolf's point of view more?

6. What do you notice about the rhyming scheme in 'Wolf'? Can you see a pattern? Describe what you notice in a few sentences.

7. Write down the meanings of the following words, as they appear in a dictionary: 'Circus Elephant': (a) *dawn* (line 2); (b) *stir* (line 14); 'Wolf': (c) *howl* (line 1); (d) *gloom* (line 3).

· ·

Precious animals

Endangered species

On January 6 2000 the last long-horned, short-haired mountain goat (*Capra pyrenaica*) died when a tree fell on it in a remote area of South-west France. That particular species is now extinct.

5 A similar fate might soon be in store for at least ten more European species, all of which are in serious decline. They include the Iberian lynx, the brown bear, the harbour porpoise, the monk seal, the marsh fritillary butterfly, the lady's slipper orchid and the corncrake. They are all in danger - not from falling trees, but of losing their natural habitats, which

10 are threatened by the sprawling tide of new roads and buildings, intensive modern farming techniques and the effects of a changing climate. Without

their homes and hunting grounds, these species will not survive.

In the last century, it is thought that at least 154 British species became
extinct. They include the short haired bumblebee, the dainty damselfly,
15   the large blue butterfly, Ivell's sea anemone and the mouse-eared bat.

Habitat loss

Human beings share
Planet Earth with an
astonishing variety of
20   other species - both
plant and animal.
But, unlike them,
we are responsible
for huge and far-
25   reaching changes
which have already
changed the face of
the earth for ever.
Forests have been
30   cut down, concrete
has replaced green
fields, land has been
poisoned by toxic
waste. The list is
35   endless. And the
result, of course, is
not only the loss of
natural habitats for
all sorts of animals,
40   birds, reptiles and
amphibians but also
the loss of precious

Iberian lynx

fertile soil. With most of the surface of the planet covered by sea, there is
only a tiny proportion of land that can provide us with the food we need
45   to survive. We must take care of it.

(From the World Wildlife Fund website at www.wwf.org.uk/gowild/planet.htm)

Exercise 6.2 ✏

Read the passages about precious animals and then answer the following questions using proper sentences.

1. How did the last short-haired mountain goat die in 2000?

2. Write down the names of three endangered species of animal in Europe.

3. Why are these European species in danger?

4. Explain in a few sentences what humans have done to forests, fields and other types of land, which leaves permanent damage and endangers animals.

5. Why is it important that we look after the earth's soil?

6. Write the meanings of the following words. You may use a dictionary to help you. (a) *endangered* (line 1); (b) *extinct* (line 4); (c) *decline* (line 6); (d) *habitat* (line 9).

. . . .

Exercise 6.3 ✏

Your turn to write:

1. Read the poem 'Circus Elephant' by Kathryn Worth again. Then write a short descriptive paragraph in which you describe another elephant roaming freely in its natural habitat.

2. Look again at 'Wolf' by Judith Nicholls. Then write a similar poem of your own about a tiger, which is afraid of being hunted for its fur.

3. Think of another animal that is endangered today – you could choose an orangutan, a blue whale, or a giant panda, for example. (You can find lots more by visiting www.wwf.org.uk). Then write an information text giving interesting facts about this animal, and explaining why it is in danger.

4. Design and produce a poster which shows the importance of saving the world's tigers. Then design a second poster for a different endangered animal. Remember to think about how you will use pictures and words to make a big impression on your readers.

5. Which are more important, humans or other animals? If every species is important, why are some allowed to become extinct? If all species share the same planet, should humans look after it more carefully? What do you think? Write down your thoughts about how we must look after the Earth, and all that's in it.

Learning about language

Pronouns (2): Possessive pronouns

You will remember from Chapter 5 how pronouns take the place of nouns. They help us to avoid repeating ourselves.

Now look at the following line from the poem 'Wolf', which contains another type of pronoun, a **possessive pronoun**.

Mine *is the howl*

The speaker in the poem is the wolf. It could also have said:

The howl is **mine**.

Either way, the word 'mine' is a possessive pronoun that tells us to whom the howl belongs. Like other types of pronoun, possessive pronouns help us to avoid repeating ourselves. Without the word 'mine' the wolf would have to say: 'The howl is my howl.'

Look at another example, using the word 'hers'.

Jane said that the book was Jane's book.

Jane said that the book was **hers**.

Note that possessive pronouns do not need an apostrophe.

Exercise 6.4 ✏️

Write a sentence for each of the following possessive pronouns to show how they are used.

1. yours   **3.** theirs   **5.** mine

2. ours   **4.** his

Exercise 6.5 ✏️

The following sentences sound odd because they contain too much repetition. Rewrite each one, using a possessive pronoun to make it tidier.

1. Henry claimed that the winning ticket was Henry's winning ticket.

2. The football team believed that victory would soon be their victory.

3. The Porsche is my Porsche.

4. Nell took Jane's picture home by mistake and left Nell's picture at school.

5. Is this pencil case your pencil case?

Belonging to...

Look at the following phrases:

The elephant's trunk   *The leopard's spots*

In these two examples we know to whom the trunk and the spots belong, because an **apostrophe** and an 's' have been added to the name of each animal – the common noun.

When we want to show to whom something belongs, we put the person's name – the proper noun – next to it, and add an **apostrophe** and an 's':

Anzar's football boots   *Jemima's violin*

Without an apostrophe, we would have to say *The football boots belonging to Anzar*, which is quite a mouthful.

Exercise 6.6 🖉

Rewrite the following phrases, using an apostrophe and an 's' to show who owns each item. Follow the example given.

Example: *the pen belonging to Mike = Mike's pen.*

1. the rucksack belonging to Tilly

2. the table belonging to Mrs Johnson

3. the motorbike belonging to Gran

4. the chocolate cake belonging to Yoseph

5. the coats belonging to the children

Remember: possessive nouns need apostrophes. Possessive pronouns do not.

Notice how the final question includes the word *children* which is a plural (more than one). Most plurals end in 's' already. If this is the case, we add an apostrophe only to show belonging. We do not add an extra 's':

the boots belonging to the players becomes *the players' boots*

. . . .

Exercise 6.7 🖉

Rewrite these phrases using an apostrophe. Some plurals will require an 's', but others will not.

1. the eggs belonging to the chickens

2. the final belonging to the men

3. the pen belonging to the sheep

4. the staff room belonging to the teachers

5. the stables belonging to the horses

Can you spell?

Collective nouns

You have read about different animals in this chapter. The animals mentioned often appear in large numbers in the wild. When we refer to these animal groups, we often use a special type of noun called a **collective noun**. Here are some examples:

a pack of wolves

a pride of lions

a herd of elephants

Words like these are not only used for animals. They can be used for people and things too:

a *crew* of sailors   a *bunch* of grapes
a *band* of musicians

Collective nouns may refer to a lot of things grouped together, but they are actually treated as singular words. So we say:

The herd is coming   rather than   *The herd are coming*

The team is going to win   rather than   *The team are going to win*

Exercise 6.8

Write out the following phrases and fill in the gaps with the right collective nouns from the list below.

flock company library shoal gang plague litter quiver

1. a _____ of soldiers

2. a _____ of sheep

3. a _____ of thieves

4. a _____ of puppies

5. a _____ of fish

6. a _____ of arrows

7. a _____ of locusts

8. a _____ of books

Exercise 6.9 ✏️

What would you expect to find in each of the following groups? Write down each collective noun and fill in the space next to it with the correct word from the words below.

pearls geese eggs bread ants flowers ships stars

1. a bouquet of _____
2. a gaggle of _____
3. a string of _____
4. a fleet of _____

5. a galaxy of _____
6. a clutch of _____
7. a batch of _____
8. a colony of _____

Speaking and listening

1. In pairs, take turns to pretend to be one of the animals in the poems at the beginning of this chapter. The other partner can ask the animal questions about how it feels, what it is afraid of and whether it thinks Man is to blame for its misery. You could perform your questions and answers in front of the class.

2. Working in small groups, imagine you have been asked to produce a two minute television advertisement for a charity that supports an endangered species of animal. You will need to give viewers information about how they can help, who they should call or write to and, most importantly, some reasons why they need to act now to save this species.

3. Carry out some research into endangered animals. You could use the Internet, books and magazines to help you. Then put together a short presentation for your class, in which you can share the information you have found. You may find it easier to focus on one or two particular species that are threatened.

4. Circle talk: In a large circle, take it in turns to discuss your favourite wild animals. Why do you like them? What is so special about them? If your favourite wild animal became extinct, how would you feel? Share your thoughts in class, then listen to others and try to respond with interesting questions and comments.

Have you read?

Each of these wonderful stories features some special animals.

The Butterfly Lion by Michael Morpurgo (Collins)
Charlotte's Web by E. B. White (Puffin Books)
Just So Stories by Rudyard Kipling (Walker Books)
The Jungle Book by Rudyard Kipling (Penguin Books)
The Wind in the Willows by Kenneth Grahame
(Penguin Books)
The Midnight Fox by Betsy Byars (Puffin Books)
The Wolves of Willoughby Chase by Joan Aiken
(Red Fox)

These books contain some fine animal poems.

A Trunkful of Elephants edited by Judith Nicholls (Methuen Children's Books)
Dragonsfire by Judith Nicholls (Faber and Faber)
Animal Kingdom Poems by Onye Kingsley (Athena Press Ltd)
Collected Animal Poems: The Iron Wolf by Ted Hughes (Faber and Faber)
Animal Poems compiled by Jennifer Curry (Scholastic Young Hippo)

Other things to do...

- Visit the BBC's Newsround website at www.news.bbc.co.uk/cbbcnews

- Look around the site and find out what it offers you. You may like to join Newsround's Press Pack Club and become a junior reporter by visiting www.bbc.co.uk/cbbc/presspack

- Find out more about zoos and how they can help prevent endangered animals from becoming extinct. Some people believe keeping animals in cages is wrong, because they belong in the wild. But others think that zoos enable us to learn about animals and appreciate how precious they are. What do *you* think?

Chapter 7

Stig of the Dump

Something, or Somebody, had a lot of shaggy black hair and two bright black eyes that were looking very hard at Barney.

'Hullo!' said Barney.

Something said nothing.

5 'I fell down the cliff,' said Barney.

Somebody grunted.

'My name's Barney.'

Somebody-Something made a noise that sounded like 'Stig'.

The Thing sitting in the corner seemed to be interested. It got up and
10 moved towards Barney into the light. Barney was glad to see it was Somebody after all.

'Funny way to dress though,' he thought, 'rabbit skins round the middle and no shoes or socks.'

'Oh puff!' said Barney, 'I can't reach my feet. You do it, Stig!'

15 He handed the knife to Stig.

Stig turned it over and felt it with his strong hairy hands, and tested the edge with a thumb. Then instead of trying to cut the creepers he squatted down on the ground and picked up a broken stone.

He's going to sharpen the knife, thought Barney.

20 But no, it seemed more as if he was sharpening the stone. Using the hard knife to chip with, Stig was carefully flaking tiny splinters off the edge of the flint, until he had a thin sharp blade. Then he sprang up, and with two or three slashes cut through the creeper that tied Barney's feet.

Barney sat up. 'Golly!' he said. 'You *are* clever! I bet my Grandad couldn't
25 do that, and he's *very* good at making things.'

Stig grinned. Then he went to the back of the cave and hid the broken knife under a pile of rubbish.

'My knife!' protested
30 Barney. But Stig took no notice. Barney got up and went into the dark part of the cave.

He'd never seen
35 anything like the collection of bits and pieces, odds and ends, bric-a-brac and old brock, that this
40 Stig creature had lying about his den. There were stones and bones, fossils and bottles, skins and
45 tins, stacks of sticks and hanks of string. There were motor-car tyres and hats from old scarecrows, nuts and bolts and bobbles from brass bedsteads.
50 There was a coal scuttle full of dead electric light bulbs and a basin with rusty screws and nails in it. There was a pile of bracken and newspapers that looked as if it were used for a bed. The place looked as if it had never been given a tidy-up.

'I wish I lived here,' said Barney.

55 Stig seemed to understand that Barney was approving of his home and his face lit up. He took on the air of a householder showing a visitor round his property, and began pointing out some of the things he seemed particularly proud of.

First, the plumbing. Where the water dripped through a crack in the
60 roof of the cave he had wedged the mud-guard of a bicycle. The water ran along this, through the tube of a vacuum-cleaner, and into a big can

with writing on it. By the side of this was a plastic football carefully cut in half, and Stig dipped up some water and offered it to Barney. Barney had swallowed a mouthful before he made out the writing on the can: it said
65   WEED KILLER. However, the water only tasted of rust and rubber.

It was dark in the back of the cave. Stig went to the front where the ashes of a fire were smoking faintly, blew on them, picked up a book that lay beside his bed, tore out a page and rolled it up, lit it at the fire, and carried it to a lamp set in a niche in the wall. As it flared up Barney could
70   see it was in fact an old teapot, filled with some kind of oil, and with a bootlace hanging out of it for a wick.

In the light of the lamp Stig went to the very back of the cave and began to thump the wall and point, and explain something in his strange grunting language. Barney did not understand a word but he recognised the tone
75   of his voice – like when grown-ups go on about: 'I'm thinking of tearing this down, and building on here, and having this done up...' Stig had been digging into the wall, enlarging his cave. There was a bit of an old bed he had been using as a pick, and a baby's bath full of loose chalk to be carried away.

80   Barney made the interested sort of noises you are supposed to make when people tell you they are going to put up plastic wallpaper with pictures of mousetraps on it, but Stig reached up to a bunch of turnips hanging from a poker stuck in the wall. He handed Barney a turnip, took one for himself, and began to eat it. Barney sat down on a bundle of old
85   magazines done up with string and munched the turnip. The turnip at least was fresh, and it tasted better to him than the cream of spinach he'd hidden under his spoon at dinner time.

Barney looked at Stig. Funny person to find living next door to you, he thought.

(From Stig of the Dump by Clive King, 1963)

Exercise 7.1 🖉

Read the passage from Clive King's *Stig of the Dump* and answer the following questions in complete sentences.

1. Why does Barney begin to call the creature 'Stig'?

2. In your own words, explain why Barney thinks Stig is clever.

3. Why do you think Barney said 'I wish I lived here'? What does Barney find so appealing about Stig's home?

4. How does Stig collect water?

5. At the end of the passage, Barney remarks that Stig is a 'funny person to find living next door to you'. Do you agree with him? Explain your answer as fully as you can.

6. Use a dictionary to find meanings for the following words: (a) *creepers* (line 17); (b) *squatted* (line 18); (c) *protested* (line 29); (d) *bracken* (line 51); (e) *niche* (line 69).

. . . .

Waste

Every year UK householders throw away the equivalent of 3 1/2 million double-decker buses (almost 30 million tonnes), a queue of which would stretch from London to Sydney, Australia and back. We all produce waste but there are things we can do to minimise how much and what impact it
5 has on our surroundings. Environmental groups tell us the way to achieve this is to 'reduce, reuse and recycle'.

A large amount of the contents of our bins is packaging which we 'buy' at the supermarket. In the UK in 2001 we produced the equivalent weight of 245 jumbo jets per week in packaging waste. Next time you are
10 shopping, think carefully about how you can **reduce** your packaging:

• take your own shopping bags so you need fewer plastic carrier bags

• buy larger containers. One larger container uses less packaging (and less energy to produce) than two small ones

• when buying apples, think whether they need to be in a plastic tray and

20   wrapped in cellophane

- buy fruit and vegetables from your local greengrocer who uses low-impact brown bags.

At home, try to think of inventive ways to **reuse** items:

- use shopping bags as bin liners

25   • take your magazines to the doctor's surgery or dentist

- take your unwanted furniture, books and clothes to a charity shop (make sure they are clean)

- use both sides of the paper in your computer printer (if you really need to print it)

30   • use plastic tubs such as margarine containers to store things or make plant pots.

More and more local councils are providing good sites for **recycling** a whole variety of goods, but there are also some things you can do at home:

35   • find out where your nearest recycling point is and what they can take – cans,
40   glass, plastic, newspapers, cardboard, shoes, old clothes

- compost all of
45   your vegetable waste, but also small quantities of shredded cardboard,
50   bedding from your pet rabbit or hamster, and grass and prunings from the garden.

All of this can make a difference: recycling just one glass bottle will save enough energy to power a television for over one hour; if collected properly, waste oil from car oil changes could supply the annual energy
55 needs of 1.5 million people; recycling aluminium cans saves 95% of the energy used in making a new can.

(Sources: www.wasteonline.org.uk and the Scottish Oil Care Campaign)

Exercise 7.2 ✏

Read the passage entitled Waste and then answer the following questions using proper sentences:

1. Write sentences to explain each of the following terms: reduce, reuse and recycle.

2. What does the writer encourage you to think about particularly when shopping?

3. Using your own words, write down two ways you can help to reduce the world's wasted packaging.

4. How can plastic tubs come in useful, according to the writer?

5. If collected properly, how much energy could be saved by recycling just three glass bottles?

6. Write down the meanings of the following words. You may use a dictionary to help you. (a) packaging (line 7); (b) cellophane (line 20); (c) inventive (line 23); (d) annual (line 54).

Exercise 7.3 ✏

Your turn to write:

1. Read the passage from Stig of the Dump again. Then continue the story in your own words. What will happen next? Will Barney and Stig find some way of communicating? Will Barney take Stig home with him to meet his family? Or will they make something together out of the bric-a-brac that lines Stig's den?

2. Rewrite the extract from *Stig of the Dump* from Stig's point of view (rather than Barney's). Use the first person narrative (*I saw a boy coming towards me...*). Describe Stig's feelings when he sees this young stranger approaching his hideaway. Will he feel threatened or excited? Angry or welcoming?

3. Can you imagine a world in which we are surrounded by litter at every corner? What would happen if we stopped recycling, if refuse collectors stopped collecting and if everyone began dropping litter on the ground? Write a descriptive paragraph describing what your town or street would be like if this were to happen. Think about the sounds, sights and smells that surround you.

4. Design a poster that tells people how they can look after the environment by recycling more. Read the article *Waste* once again to remind you what can be done. Then put its advice on your poster, with pictures and powerful messages to catch people's attention and make them stop and think.

· ·

Learning about language

Speech marks

Look at the following line from *Stig of the Dump*:

'I fell down the cliff,' said Barney.

Here we can see what Barney actually says to Stig. There are **speech marks** or inverted commas either side of the spoken words.

In most printed books today you will find that the speech marks are single strokes (' and '). But in handwritten stories, you will usually find two: " and ". Either way is correct, but you should be consistent.

If you want to show what characters are actually saying to one another, or if you wish to quote real people in a report, for example, then you must put speech marks around their spoken words. This is called **direct speech** because you are quoting directly from the person speaking.

Exercise 7.4

Write out each of these sentences, adding speech marks, either singles or doubles, in the correct places:

1. Hullo! said Barney.

2. Oh puff! said Barney, I can't reach my feet. You do it, Stig!

3. My knife! protested Barney.

4. I wish I lived here, said Barney.

5. Golly! he said. You *are* clever! I bet my Grandad couldn't do that, and he's *very* good at making things.

You can write direct speech in several different ways:

The spoken words can come at the beginning of the sentence:

   'Gosh! What a lot of junk you have!' said Barney.

Or they can come at the end of the sentence:

   Barney said, 'Gosh! What a lot of junk you have!'

Or even at both ends:

   'Gosh!' said Barney, 'What a lot of junk you have!'

Whichever way you choose, remember that the speech marks come after the punctuation (e.g. full stop, exclamation mark or comma).

Exercise 7.5

Rewrite these sentences so that all the spoken words come at the beginning of each one. Look back at the example above for help.

1. Barney said, 'I've made a new friend today.'

2. 'David!' cried Mum, 'Don't leave your litter on the floor!'

3. Mum asked, 'Have you washed your hands after your adventures?'

4. The park attendant said, 'Please do not leave crisp packets on the grass.'

5. 'Mr Stig,' whispered Barney, 'Do you like living in this cave?'

Imperatives

Look again at the article entitled Waste. You will see that it contains many bullet points. Each one offers some advice or instructions on how to reduce waste

Here are some extracts from the article:

take *your own shopping bags...*

buy *fruit and vegetables from your local greengrocer...*

use *both sides of the paper in your computer printer...*

The words in blue are highlighted for a special reason. They are **imperatives**. These are verbs which invite or order someone to do something.

Many instructions begin with imperative verbs. Look at these:

Stir *in the milk.* **Mix** *the batter.* (recipes)

Turn *right, then* **take** *the second turning on the left.* (directions)

Leave *all belongings and* **proceed** *to the nearest exit.* (instructions)

. . . .

Exercise 7.6 ✏

Write each of the following sentences adding a suitable imperative from the words below:

call screw turn put relax mix

I. At the end of the road _____ right.

2. _____ the flour and water together to make a paste.

3. After fitting the drawers, _____ the handles onto the front.

4. In an emergency _____ 999.

5. _____ all items of litter in the bins provided.

6. _____ in our luxury Jacuzzi.

Exercise 7.7

Write (an imperative!) a suitable sentence of your own for each of the
following imperatives:

1. take	**3.** press	**5.** keep off
2. close	**4.** ask	**6.** write

Can you spell?

i before **e**

There are many words in the English language that
contain the letter patterns *ie* or *ei*. Here are some examples:

gr**ie**f	ch**ie**f	bel**ie**f
eight	w**ei**gh	sl**ei**gh

So far so good. These are quite easy to remember because the **ie** words all
have an 'ee' sound while the **ei** words shown here have an 'ay' sound.

Exercise 7.8

Write these words filling in the missing letters with either **ie** or **ei**. Think
about the sounds that the words make when you try adding each letter
pattern in turn.

1. ___ ghteen	**4.** bel___ ve
2. w___ ght	**5.** n___ ghbour
3. th___ f	**6.** pr___ st

The sound of these words (and their appearance) should be familiar to you.
However, as you might expect, there are some exceptions. For example, the
word **receive** has an 'ee' sound, but look closely: it actually has the letters
ei in it. This is because the letters **ei** follow the letter **c**, and it follows a rule
which you may have heard:

'**i** before **e** except after **c**.'

Exercise 7.9 ✏️

Find out the meanings of the following *ei* words and then write a sentence containing each one. Remember to spell them correctly.

1. receipt   3. deceit   5. ceiling

2. perceive   4. conceited

So the complete rule for you to learn with words of this kind is:

i comes before **e** – *fie*ld except after **c** – *cei*ling

or when the sound is not 'ee'– w*ei*gh

· ·

Speaking and listening

1. Hot seating: Take turns to sit in a chair at the front of the class as either Stig or Barney from *Stig of the Dump*. Invite the rest of the class to ask you questions about how you felt during your first meeting at Stig's den.

2. In pairs, act out a small scene in which you play the parts of Stig and his new friend Barney. Read the passage again and try to use as much of the same language as possible.

3. Work in groups of three or four. Read together the article called Waste. Then put together a short presentation for the class on how to look after the environment by recycling and being careful with litter.

4. Talk for one minute: Look again at the passage from *Stig of the Dump*. Pay special attention to all the items in Stig's dump. Then take turns to speak for one minute on any of the bits of rubbish that Stig has collected. Try to avoid saying that familiar word 'erm' or repeating yourself.

Have you read?

The following books are all about rubbish and the art of recycling.

Where does Rubbish Go? by S. Tahta (Usborne Publishing Ltd)
Rubbish and Recycling by Stephanie Turnbull (Usborne Publishing Ltd)
Why Should I Recycle? by Jen Green (Hodder Wayland)
I Can Help Recycle Our Rubbish by V. Smith (Franklin Watts Ltd)
Make it with Rubbish by Anna Llimos Plomer (Book House)
The Art of Recycling by Laura C. Martin (Storey Books)
Awesome Things to Make with Recycled Stuff by Heather Smith
(Sterling Juvenile)
The Stinking Story of Rubbish by Katie Daynes (Usborne Publishing Ltd)
Billy Rubbish by Alexander McCall Smith (Mammoth)
Henry's Leg by Ann Pilling (Puffin Books)

Other things to do...

- Have you ever made something special from bits of old rubbish? Perhaps a model castle, using old boxes? Or a jewellery box? Write a set of instructions to show someone how to make something useful from the spare items lying around the house. You could choose: a den, a cricket set, a miniature horsebox or stable, a robot or even a rocket, for example. Try to think of new and exciting ways to use the bric-a-brac in your house and garage.

- Find out more about how recycling is helping us to clean up and look after our world. You can find lots more information at the following websites: www.recycle-more.co.uk
www.recyclenow.com
www.actionfornature.org

Chapter 8

Crabs Walk Sideways

Scuttling through cluttered
neighbourhoods, in tepid pools
and salty shadows.

Racing ripples across sun-scorched
5 lime. Limbs clatter on rock.

Clicking quickly to avoid
the crunch
of a passing boot.

Burrowing deep
10 in sludgy sediment
for hapless molluscs.

Dancing on mudflats,
a clattering tango.

Carrying the shopping
15 home.

Andrew Hammond

Exercise 8.1 ✏

Read the poem entitled 'Crabs Walk Sideways' by Andrew Hammond and
then answer the following questions in complete sentences:

1. The word neighbourhoods is usually used to describe areas where lots
of people live near one another. Why do you think the poet has chosen
to use it in a poem about crabs on a beach?

2. What do you think is meant by 'the crunch of a passing boot'?

3. There are lots of words that have the letter pattern **cl** in them – like
cluttered, **cl**atter, **cl**icking and **cl**attering. Can you think of a reason why
the poet has chosen to use these words in this poem?

4. Do you think sludgy is a good word to describe the sediment or wet sand that lies near the water's edge? Give reasons for your answer.

5. Do crabs actually dance? Why do you think the poet uses the word dancing in this poem?

6. Use a dictionary to find meanings for the following words: (a) *tepid* (line 2); (b) *hapless* (line 11); (c) *molluscs* (line 11); (d) *mudflats* (line 12); (e) *tango* (line 13).

· ·

Crusty crab

Pie-crust crabs are well named, because the top part of their
5 shell, called the carapace, looks just like the pastry lid of a pie. These crabs spend much
10 of their time hiding under rocks or seaweed, and they are much less aggressive than
15 their relatives, the velvet crabs.

Pie-crust crabs eat small animals, such as shrimps
20 and mussels. They are also great scavengers, eating the remains of dead creatures that they find in the rock pool. Adult pie-crust crabs can grow to measure more than 15 cm across the shell. The little crabs that you see in rock pools are still very young. As they grow, they move down the shore into deeper water. A pie-crust crab can live for eight years or

25 more, but the female does not lay eggs until she is about five years old. She may lay more than three million eggs during her lifetime, but only a few will survive to grow into adults.

Hairy legs

The crab's legs are hairy. These hairs, called setae, are very sensitive. They
30 help the crab to feel its way around as it climbs over seaweed, and into dark cracks and crevices in the rock.

Raising the roof

The crab's body is well protected by its hard outer shell, called the exoskeleton. Like shrimps, lobsters, and other crustaceans, the crab
35 moults (sheds) its exoskeleton every few weeks as it grows, revealing a new one underneath. To get out of the old shell, the crab swallows so much water that the top part of the shell is forced away from the bottom part. The crab then pulls itself out backwards.

(From Rock Pool (Look Closer Series) by Christiane Gunzi, 1998)

Exercise 8.2

1. Explain, in your own words, how pie-crust crabs got their name.

2. If you found a pie-crust crab in a rock pool how would you know that it was only a young one?

3. Only a tiny proportion of the female's eggs grow into adults. What do you think happens to the rest?

4. Describe in your own words the extraordinary way in which the crab sheds its old shell.

5. In what way are 'setae' useful to the pie-crust crab?

6. Write definitions for the following words: (a) *aggressive* (line 14); (b) *scavengers* (line 20); (c) *crevice* (line 31); (d) *exoskeleton* (line 34).

Exercise 8.3 ✏

Your turn to write:

1. Choose another sea creature that you might find on a beach and describe it in a poem of your own. Think about the sound of the words you use, as well as the meaning. You might want to choose from the following: jellyfish, barnacle, seagull, periwinkle, shrimp, lobster.

2. Write a short story in which someone makes an exciting discovery on a beach. Perhaps it is a new type of creature, a message in a bottle, or even some buried treasure. Remember to describe the setting in as much detail as you can.

3. Put together a 'factfile' on a particular sea creature. Use the Internet, encyclopaedias and magazines. Include its appearance, where it lives, what it eats, how many eggs it lays, and its lifespan.

· ·

Learning about language
Alliteration

Look again at the title of the second passage: 'Crusty crab'.

These words begin with the same sound: **cr**

When two or more words beginning with the same sound are placed together, we call it **alliteration**. Many writers, from newspaper journalists to poets, use alliteration to make their writing sound more appealing. Here are some other examples of alliteration, with suggestions for where you might find them:

Delicious Doughnuts (a menu)
Salty Seaweed (a seaside poem)
Magnificent Manchester United Make it to Final (a newspaper)

Exercise 8.4 ✏

Write two or more adjectives to accompany each of the following seaside words, and make an alliterative phrase. Follow the example given.

Example: *crab – crazy, creepy crabs*

1. shell
2. beach
3. lobster
4. barnacles
5. jellyfish
6. rock pool

Exercise 8.5 ✏

Now write a whole sentence for each of these animals. Include some alliteration in each one. Here is another example for you to follow.

Example: *dolphin – Through the waves the dolphin darted.*

1. tiger
2. whale
3. octopus
4. wolf
5. snake
6. chimpanzee

Prepositions

Look at the following lines from the poem, 'Crabs Walk Sideways':

> *Scuttling **through** cluttered*
> *neighbourhoods, **in** tepid pools*
> *and salty shadows.*
> *Racing ripples **across** sun-scorched*
> *lime. Limbs clatter **on** rock.*

The words highlighted in blue are **prepositions**. They tell us the **position** one thing has in relation to another. The crabs are scuttling **through** the cluttered neighbourhoods. Their limbs are clattering **on** the rocks.

The boy tiptoed into the sea.

The boy	tiptoed	into	the sea
noun	**verb**	**preposition**	**noun**

There are many different prepositions. Some examples include:

across   near   below   above   off   on

Remember: a **preposition** tells you the **position** one thing has in relation to another. This could mean its physical position or where it comes in time: e.g. **before** or **after**.

Exercise 8.6

Write sentences to show the meanings of each of the following prepositions.

1. towards   **4.** against

2. before   **5.** upon

3. after

Exercise 8.7

Write the following sentences and fill in the gaps with a suitable preposition from the words below:

through beside onto under at into

1. They sat _____ the river and ate their picnic.

2. When they arrived ____ the beach, Mike and Aziz ran _____ the sea.

3. 'Don't walk _____ the woods alone,' said Aunt Jane.

4. Mary did not like the hot sun, so she found a nice shady spot _____ a large tree.

5. Excited about their day trip, the children climbed eagerly _____ the coach.

Can you spell?

More common endings: -en or -on?

Many words end in **-en** or **-on**. The problem is they sound similar. Say the following words out loud and notice how their endings sound the same.

sudden   button

Choosing the wrong ending is a very common mistake. But there is one easy rule you can remember for most, though not all, words of this type.

Most words that end in **-on** are nouns.

prison   lemon   mutton

But most words that end in **-en** are either verbs or adjectives. The letters **-en** have been added to root words to turn them into verbs and adjectives, for example:

damp   dampen   gold   golden

As always there are exceptions. Just think of a kitten.

· ·

Exercise 8.8 ✏

Write the following sentences and complete the word underlined with the correct ending. You may need to check your spelling in a dictionary before you finish.

1. 'Is this seat tak___?' asked the lady on the bus.

2. I met a very helpful pers___ in the supermarket.

3. Julie said she had been bitt___ by a mosquito.

4. After a long day in the garden, Grandpa's back was beginning to stiff___.

5. The Christmas seas___ is nearly upon us.

Exercise 8.9 ✏️

Find five words that end in **–en** and five ending with **–on** in the following wordsearch. Write them in your book.

d	l	k	o	q	m	c	e	i	t
o	m	a	n	e	t	s	a	f	h
p	j	u	k	v	x	i	t	i	n
a	k	i	t	t	e	n	a	o	e
n	e	y	o	t	e	g	s	g	t
o	q	w	l	v	o	i	u	e	t
s	d	l	e	m	o	n	d	k	i
a	b	s	w	p	j	o	d	z	b
e	c	n	o	t	e	l	e	k	s
s	d	a	j	h	m	o	n	p	u

Speaking and listening

1. Take turns in class to read out your poems about sea creatures. Try to learn your own poem by heart. This will help you to perform it in a lively way, without having to look down at your work.

2. In groups of about three, play a game of charades in which each person takes a turn in miming a sea creature to the group, using silent actions only. It should be interesting to see what sort of actions you perform to help your friends guess what you are thinking of.

3. Talk for one minute: Take turns in class to talk for a minute about a specific sea creature. Try to avoid repeating yourself or hesitating and saying 'erm'!

4. Test your memory by playing a circle game in which each person takes a turn to say the following line, each time adding a new animal to the end: *I went down to the rising tide and when I was there I spied a _____ (e.g. jellyfish, pie-crust crab).* How many animals will you be able to remember as you take turns around the circle?

Have you read?

The following books contain lots of interesting poems about the sea and the seashore.

Sea Dream: Poems from Under the Waves by Nikki Siegen-Smith (Barefoot Books)
Sailing Days: Stories and Poems about Sailors and the Sea by Amy McKay (Antique Collectors Club Children's Classics)
Poems of the Sea (Everyman's Library Pocket Poets) by J. D. McClatchy (Everyman's Library)
Under the Moon and Over the Sea by John Agard (Candlewick Press)
Sea Poems: A Seafarer Anthology by Bob Crew (Sheridan House)
The Dragon Book of Verse by Michael Harrison (Oxford University Press)
Seaside Poems by Jill Bennett (Oxford University Press)

These encyclopedias contain some interesting information about the sea.

Coral Reef: Around the Clock with the Animals of the Ocean (24 Hours series) (Dorling Kindersley Publishers Ltd)
Great British Marine Animals by Paul Naylor (Sound Diving Publications)
Rock Pool (Look Closer Series) by Christine Gunzi (Dorling Kindersley Limited)
Shoreline (Look Closer Series) by Barbara Taylor (Dorling Kindersley Limited)
At the Seaside: What was it like in the past? by Louise Spilsbury (Heinemann Library)

Other things to do...

- Crabs are fascinating creatures. Did you know, for example, that each November, on a tiny island near Australia, over 100 million tiny crabs crawl right through the homes and gardens of the islanders to reach the coast? Use the Internet, books and magazines to find out more about this world-famous event.

- Make your own spyglass for dipping in rock pools and watching crabs. All you need is a small bucket and some clear plastic. Ask an adult to cut out the bottom of the bucket. Then fasten a round piece of clear plastic to the base using tape or glue. Push the bucket into the water and you can see the bottom.

- Crabs walk sideways, as the poem says, but what other animals have unusual walks? Can you think of any? Use the Internet, encyclopaedias and magazines to find other examples of creatures with strange ways of getting about, and then amuse your friends with impressions of them.

Chapter 9

Together at last

After years of war and a dangerous journey from Poland to the safety of Switzerland, Ruth Ballicki is thrilled to find her parents, at last.

It was dark when Ruth opened her eyes. She was being lifted up.

A man's voice said, 'It's a girl – thin as a string of seaweed and wringing wet. How you feeling, eh? We nearly ran you down in the dark.'

He spoke in a strange language which Ruth did not understand. She tried
5   to speak, but no words came.

'She's worrying about something,' said the man.

'Better take her below and get some dry clothes on her,' said someone else.

Her mind drifted to a blank.

10   When she woke again, she was lying in a bunk. There was a light above her, dry blankets round her, and a flicker of warmth in her limbs.

'Where am I?' she said.

Strange faces peered down at her from the sky. There was a cup at her lips.

15   'Feed her slowly,' a man was saying. 'Don't give her too much or she'll be sick.'

The cup came back again, and biscuits too. She sat up.

'Edek! Bronia! Jan!' she cried.

'Polish names,' said a woman's voice. 'I said she was Polish. Anyone talk
20   Polish?' And Ruth, frightened by the unfamiliar faces, cried out again, 'Edek! Bronia! Jan!'

And suddenly from the back of the crowd came the echo, 'Edek! Bronia! Jan!' in a deep voice. Dazed and bewildered though she was, she knew it for her father's voice. Now she was gathered in his arms, smothered with
25   his kisses. She tried to speak, to listen to what he was saying. But her head

was throbbing and she was too tired to keep her eyes open.

When she woke again, her father's face was close to hers.

'You've been asleep a long time,' he said. 'Try to stay awake and I'll show you what you want to see.'

30 The blankets pressed round her and she felt herself being lifted from the bunk.

'Look down there,' said Joseph.

She saw, in a nest of blankets, Bronia's sleeping head. There was a flush of colour on the child's cheeks and she was snoring.

35 'Nothing much wrong with her,' said Joseph, and he carried Ruth to the next bunk.

She looked again and saw Edek's face. It was very white, and
40 he was lying still and as straight as a post.

'Is he breathing?' she said.

'Yes, he's breathing,'
45 said Joseph, 'but only just.' And he carried her quickly away and showed her Jan.

He was sitting on his
50 blankets, dangling his legs over the edge of the bunk. There was a glint of mischief in his eyes.

55 'They're a feeble lot, the Ballickis,' he said.

'They would all have drowned if it hadn't been for me. Ruth, you're crazy. Fancy going for a sail in weather like this – and thinking you could manage without me! You use an oar like a soup spoon, and when a little water
60 comes in the boat you faint. I had to find Edek's boat and steer ours to it. I shouted to him to help, but he fainted too. The water was nearly up to his neck. So I pulled him over the side into our boat – two seconds before his turned over and sank.'

Joseph patted his cheek affectionately. 'Eat up your bread and cheese and
65 stop boasting,' he said. 'If you say any more, you'll go off pop.'

Ruth reached out her arms to Jan and gave him a hug. 'You ought to be made an admiral at once,' she said. 'Thank God they're safe, all three of them.' And then she flung her arms round her father's neck.

'You've got your numbers wrong. I haven't finished yet. Hey, don't strangle
70 me!' he said. And he carried her out of the cabin.

'There are only three,' said Ruth. 'What do you mean?'

'The last and best surprise,' said Joseph, opening another door. 'I tried to tell you over the phone, but I couldn't make myself heard.'

The cabin was small, and there was only one person in it. She had been
75 waiting for the door to open. Her eyes were wide with expectation, her arms stretched out in welcome.

'Mother!' said Ruth, and with a happiness that no words can describe she slipped from her father's arms into those other arms, so eager to receive her.

(From The Silver Sword by Ian Serraillier, 1956)

Exercise 9.1

Read the passage from *The Silver Sword*. Then answer the following questions in complete sentences:

1. How can you tell that Ruth does not know where she is when she wakes up for the second time?

2. How do the strangers know that Ruth is Polish?

3. In what way is Jan boastful?

4. The author says that Ruth greeted her mother with 'a happiness that no words can describe'. Put those feelings into words for Ruth, in a sentence or two.

5. Describe the character of Ruth's father from the evidence you can find in this passage.

6. Use a dictionary to find meanings for the following words: (a) *bewildered* (line 23); (b) *smothered* (line 24); (c) *mischief* (line 53); (d) *eager* (line 78).

Anne Frank's hideaway

Brave Anne

The story of how brave, thirteen-year old Anne Frank lived in hiding in Amsterdam to escape the Nazis is well-known across the world. To keep her spirits up during such a difficult time, she kept a diary.

Wednesday 23rd February 1944

Dear Kitty,

It's lovely weather outside and I've quite perked up since yesterday. Nearly every morning I go to the attic where Peter works, to blow the stuffy air out of my lungs.
5 From my favourite spot on the floor I look up at the blue sky and the bare chestnut tree, on whose branches little raindrops glisten like silver, and at the seagulls and other birds as they glide on the wind.

He stood with his head against a thick beam, and I sat down. We breathed the fresh air, looked outside and both felt that the spell should not be broken by words. We
10 remained like this for a long time, and when he had to go up to the loft to chop wood, I knew that he was a nice fellow. He climbed the ladder, and I followed; then he chopped wood for about a quarter of an hour, during which time we still remained silent. I watched him from where I stood; he was obviously doing his best to show off his strength. But I looked out of the open window too, over a large area of
15 Amsterdam, over all the roofs and on to the horizon, which was such a pale blue that it was hard to see the dividing line. 'As long as this exists,' I thought, 'and I may live to see it, this sunshine, the cloudless skies, while this lasts, I cannot be unhappy.'

The best remedy for those who are afraid, lonely or unhappy is to go outside, somewhere they can be quiet, alone with the heavens, nature and God. Because only
20 then does one feel that all is as it should be and that God wishes to see people happy, amidst the simple beauty of nature. As long as this exists, and it certainly always will, I know that then there will always be comfort for every sorrow, whatever the circumstances may be. And I firmly believe that nature brings solace in all troubles.

Oh, who knows, perhaps it won't be long before I can share this overwhelming
25 feeling of bliss with someone who feels the way I do about it.

Yours,
ANNE.

(From The Diary of Anne Frank by Anne Frank, 1947)

Exercise 9.2 ✏️

Read the passage from *The Diary of Anne Frank*, then answer the following questions in complete sentences:

1. What reason does Anne give for visiting the attic most mornings?

2. What do you think Anne means by the word 'spell' in the following sentence?

   'We breathed the fresh air, looked outside and both felt that the spell should not be broken by words.'

3. Why was it hard for Anne to see the dividing line where the sky meets the horizon?

4. Anne Frank was actually living in very cramped conditions, hiding from the German soldiers, yet she seems happy in this passage. What cheers her up?

5. Describe Anne's character from the evidence you have in this passage. What sort of person is she?

6. Use a dictionary to find meanings for the following words: (a) *perked* (line 3); (b) *remedy* (line 18); (c) *solace* (line 23); (d) *bliss* (line 25).

. . . .

Exercise 9.3 ✏️

Your turn to write:

1. Write a story in which you and your family have to make a very long and difficult journey away from your home because of the threat of war. Describe the journey to safety and the dangers along the way. Then describe how you feel when you finally reach safety.

2. Read the first passage again. Then rewrite it from the point of view of Joseph Ballicki, Ruth's father. Try to describe the action as he sees it, starting with Ruth waking up to the moment when at last she greets her mother. Remember to describe his feelings about having his family back together again.

3. What do you know about evacuation? Have you learned anything about the Second World War at school? Produce a short piece of writing in which you explain what you know about how and why people were evacuated during the Second World War.

4. Have you ever kept a diary? Find yourself a nice notebook – one which you will enjoy writing neatly in. Then begin keeping a diary in which you record the events of your day and your reactions to them. You don't need to show anyone your work. It can be a secret diary just for you.

Learning about language

Adverbs

Adverbs help to describe the action in a sentence. They **add** details to the **verb**.

Many adverbs (but not all) are formed by adding the letters **–ly** to an adjective like these examples from the first passage:

'Feed her **slowly**,' a man was saying. (Adjective = slow)

Joseph patted his cheek **affectionately**. (Adjective = affectionate)

In the first example, the adverb **slowly** shows us **how** Ruth needs to be fed. In the second, with the help of the adverb **affectionately**, we can see that Joseph patted Jan's cheek **in a caring sort of way**. Both adverbs answer the question **how?** and are called adverbs of manner. We also use adverbs of time which answer the question **when?** For example, **soon** and **now**. Finally, we use adverbs to answer the question **where?** For example, **here** and **there**.

Exercise 9.4

Write a sentence using each of the following adverbs.

1. usually	4. patiently	7. here	10. often
2. quickly	5. excitedly	8. now	
3. angrily	6. soon	9. there	

Exercise 9.5

Write each of the following sentences, filling the gaps with an appropriate adverb from the box below.

> happily   jealously   here   slowly   fast

1. I _____ realised that I was being watched.

2. David stared _____ at Harry's new football.

3. Jane had to run _____ to catch up with her friends.

4. The place was quiet when we arrived _____.

5. When the final exam finished, I danced _____ out of the room.

. . . .

Capital letters

Think of the different reasons for using a capital letter. Look at the following sentence from the second passage. The capital letters have been changed. Can you remember where they should be?

'nothing much wrong with her,' said joseph, and he carried ruth to the next bunk.

You should have found three missing letters:

- at the beginning of the sentence (**N**othing)

- for each name or proper noun (**J**oseph and **R**uth). Capital letters are used:

  - to begin sentences
  - for titles and headings
  - for people's names
  - to show when someone begins speaking
  - when using the first person 'I'
  - for the names of places
  - for the days of the week and months of the year.

Exercise 9.6 ✏️

Write the following sentences taken from the two passages. Change small letters to capitals wherever you think it is necessary:

1. it was dark when ruth opened her eyes.

2. 'where am i?' she said.

3. ruth reached out her arms to jan and gave him a hug.

4. nearly every morning I go to the attic where peter works to blow the stuffy air out of my lungs.

5. but I looked out of the open window too, over a large area of amsterdam.

. . . .

Exercise 9.7 ✏️

Rewrite the following passage, taken from another part of *The Silver Sword*. Put in all the necessary capital letters.

chapter 14

city of the lost

it was the end of may when the train reached berlin – after nine days of stopping and starting, of lying up in sidings, of crawling along the battered track.

the station was a shambles, but everyone was glad to escape from the cramped quarters. they swarmed out of the trucks into the dusty ruins of berlin.

Can you spell?

-sion and -tion

The letter patterns **–sion** and **–tion** are used in many different words. The problem for us is that they sound very similar, so it is not always clear which one is right.

Look at these examples:

pension   *attention*

extension   *relation*

All of these words have a 'shun' sound at the end. One thing is certain – this sound is rarely spelt with a **sh** as in fa**sh**ion.

If there is a **c** just before the 'shun' sound, then it is always spelled with **–tion**, e.g.

*se**c**tion*   *attra**c**tion*   *conne**c**tion*

Exercise 9.8

Write the following sentences, adding the missing letters to the key words. You may need to check your answers in a dictionary before finishing.

1. It was a special occa_ion and Mum was baking a cake.

2. This afternoon we completed some comprehen_ion work.

3. I listened carefully to my instruc_ions.

4. We soon realised that we were driving in the wrong direc_ion!

5. Without the right revi_ion, I will be unable to pass the examina_ion.

Exercise 9.9

Write dictionary definitions for the following words:

1. concussion
2. evaporation
3. circulation
4. concession
5. suction

6. destruction
7. excursion
8. pension
9. function
10. diversion

Speaking and listening

1. Role-play: In small groups, take turns to play the role of one of the characters in the first passage, perhaps Ruth or Joseph Ballicki. Invite others in your group to question you about where you have come from and how you feel. If you do not know the story of *The Silver Sword*, you can make up some adventures for your character.

2. Read the first passage again. Then work with a group of friends to put on a short play version of what happens in the passage. You can take a role each and act the scene, beginning with the moment when Ruth wakes up to find herself surrounded by strangers.

3. Find out more about the brave girl called Anne Frank. When you have more information about her, put together a short talk for your class (or for your parents at home). Describe her character and the things she had to cope with during her short life.

4. In her diary, Anne Frank suggests that 'the best remedy for people who are afraid, lonely or unhappy is to go outside and be quiet, alone with the heavens, nature and God'. Do you agree? How do you cheer yourself up when you are feeling sad? In small discussion groups, share your thoughts.

Have you read?

The following stories and non-fiction books tell tales of hardship and bravery during wartime, beginning with a younger reader's version of *The Diary of Anne Frank*.

Anne Frank, the Last Days of Freedom by Roy Apps (Hodder Children's Books)
When Hitler Stole Pink Rabbit by Judith Kerr (Collins)
Goodnight Mister Tom by Michelle Magorian (Puffin Books)
I am David by Anne Holm (Mammoth)
The Machine Gunners by Robert Westall (Macmillan Children's Books)
Refugee Boy by Benjamin Zephaniah (Bloomsbury)
No Turning Back by Beverley Naidoo (Puffin Books)
Evacuation (History Detective Investigates: Britain at War Series) by Martin Parsons (Hodder Wayland)
Children and the Blitz by Jane Shuter (Heinemann Library)
A Wartime Childhood by Faye Gardner (Evans Brothers – Books for Children)

Other things to do...

- Anne Frank and her family found a place to hide in Amsterdam during much of the war. Do you know where this is? Do you know how many countries were directly involved in the Second World War? Do some research to find out which countries of the world were affected by the Second World War. You may be surprised to see how many there were.

- Find a copy of *The Silver Sword* by Ian Serraillier. Once you have read it, write a review of the story, describing what you think of the plot, setting and characters. Would you recommend it to someone else? You can see another review of this book by visiting www.k-d-i-evans.demon.co.uk/ibkr65.htm

- Find out more about the life of Anne Frank by visiting the following websites: www.annefrank.com; www.annefrank.org.uk

Chapter 10

The Iron Man

The Iron Man came to the top of the cliff.

How far had he walked? Nobody knows. Where had he come from?
Nobody knows. How was he made? Nobody knows.

Taller than a house, the Iron Man stood at the top of the cliff, on the very
5   brink, in the darkness.

The wind sang through his iron fingers. His great iron head, shaped like a
dustbin but as big as a bedroom, slowly turned to the right, slowly turned
to the left. His iron ears turned, this way, that way. He was hearing
the sea. His eyes, like headlamps, glowed white, then red, then infra-red,
10 searching the sea. Never before had the Iron Man seen the sea.

He swayed
in the strong
wind that
pressed
15 against his
back. He
swayed
forward, on
the brink of
20 the high cliff.

And his right
foot, his
enormous
iron right foot,
25 lifted – up, out,
into space,
and the Iron
Man stepped
forward, off
30 the cliff, into
nothingness.

CRRRAAAASSSSSSSH!

Down the cliff the Iron Man came toppling, head over heels.

CRASH!

35 CRASH!

CRASH!

From rock to rock, snag to snag, tumbling slowly. And as he crashed and crashed and crashed

His iron legs fell off.

40 His iron arms broke off, and the hands broke off the arms.

His great iron ears fell off and his eyes fell out.

His great iron head fell off.

All the separate pieces tumbled, scattered, crashing, bumping, clanging, down on to the rocky beach far below.

45 A few rocks tumbled with him.

Then

Silence.

Only the sound of the sea, chewing away at the edge of the rocky beach, where the bits and pieces of the Iron Man lay scattered far and wide, 50 silent and unmoving.

Only one of the iron hands, lying beside an old, sand-logged washed-up seaman's boot, waved its fingers for a minute, like a crab on its back. Then it lay still.

While the stars went on wheeling through the sky and the wind went 55 on tugging at the grass on the cliff-top and the sea went on boiling and booming.

(From The Iron Man by Ted Hughes, 1968)

Exercise 10.1 ✏️

Read the passage from *The Iron Man* and answer the following questions in complete sentences:

1. What do you think is meant by the sentence: The wind sang through his iron fingers (line 6)?

2. Is this the first time the Iron Man has seen the sea?

3. What happened to the Iron Man during his fall from the cliff top?

4. Where did one of his hands end up?

5. In lines 2 to 3 Ted Hughes asks a series of questions about the Iron Man. Read them again and then answer each one, offering your own views and suggestions. Remember to use your imagination.

6. Ted Hughes is famous for the rich and exciting descriptive language he uses in his stories and poems. Which line did you particularly enjoy here, and why?

6. Use a dictionary to find the meanings of the following words:
   (a) *brink* (line 5); (b) *infra-red* (line 9); (c) *snag* (line 37); (d) *wheeling* (line 54).

· ·

The Obedient Robot

Clare Wojciechowski remembers her extraordinary encounter as a child, in the 1930s, with a 'real' Iron Man...

I vividly remember when I was just seven years old, my father took me to a demonstration, which was held at the Drill Hall in Swansea, belonging to the Territorial Army.

Posters displayed over Swansea had emblazoned in large black letters:
5 'THE IRON MAN – he walks, he sits, and he obeys commands.' This was in the 1930s, long before robots, computers, or space travel were ever thought of.

Crowds flocked to the demonstration at the hall. I remember my father sat on the end of the row near the centre aisle with myself at his side.

10 In front was a raised platform with closed curtains arousing much curiosity, and an excited buzz of conversation filled the hall. Suddenly there was silence as the curtains opened slowly, followed by 'Ahhh...'. I clung close to my father, as right in centre stage was a great metal chair and sitting upon it was the huge figure of a man made of gleaming black

15 iron.

In his square-shaped head were small slits for eyes, which were lit and seemed to flicker; there was no nose but a larger slit for a mouth. Where his ears should have been were, what I now understand to be antennae, his great arms were jointed at the shoulder and elbow, his large heavy

20 torso had a small door in the centre of his chest.

His legs were jointed at the hips and knees, and he wore great black iron boots. A truly terrifying sight!

The inventor of the machine came on stage saying that he was a professor and inventor and would now give a demonstration as to what the iron

25 man could do.

The professor spoke into a large microphone and said, 'Stand up!'

There was no response, and then he explained that it was only when he used a certain phrase that the iron man would respond. The professor then said, 'I command you to stand.'

30 Immediately the great bulk creaked and stood a full seven feet or more. Again there were 'Ahhhs...' from the audience.

The professor then gave several more commands, interspersing them with false ones to demonstrate. The iron man lifted each of his arms in turn, and each knee bent to the commands.

35 Then – and this is what I remember most of all – the inventor commanded him to walk; there was a ramp leading from the stage into the centre aisle where we sat!

As the great figure moved slowly and ponderously toward us, with his eyes flickering like two bright candles, each step resounding on the

40 wooden floor I buried my face in my father's coat afraid to look! Soon the command came to 'Turn' and 'Walk'; the giant man returned to the

stage and after the command to 'Sit', was switched off by the professor.

I must have been very frightened despite assurances from my father, as I have never forgotten this happening.

(Originally from the BBC website for the South West)

Exercise 10.2 🖊

Read the passage entitled 'The Obedient Robot'. Answer the following questions in complete sentences:

1. Why was it particularly surprising to see a poster about an iron man who 'walks, sits and obeys commands' in the 1930s?

2. Why would closed curtains make an audience curious?

3. Using the description offered in the passage, draw an accurate sketch of the iron man to show what it looked like.

4. Why did the iron man refuse to obey the professor's first request to stand?

5. Describe the other actions that the iron man performed for the professor whilst on stage.

6. Do you think the iron man was a real robot? Explain your answer as fully as you can.

7. Use a dictionary to help you find the meanings of the following words: (a) *emblazoned* (line 4); (b) *demonstration* (line 8); (c) *antennae* (line 18); (d) *interspersing* (line 32); (e) *ponderously* (line 38).

Exercise 10.3 ✏

Your turn to write:

1. You may remember that in an acrostic poem the first letter of the first word on each line can be read downwards to form a word. Write your own acrostic poem using the words IRON MAN running down the margin. Try to describe the appearance and personality of the Iron Man in the story by Ted Hughes.

2. What happens next in the story? If you know the story of *The Iron Man* quite well, write a summary of what happens in the next scene. If you do not, then write what you think might happen next in the story.

3. Imagine being in the audience at the Drill Hall in Swansea, when the professor first demonstrated his 'Iron Man'. You are sitting near to Clare Wojciechowski. Describe the show and your reactions to it. Will you believe the iron man is 'real'?

4. Do you think we shall all be using robots in our houses in the future? Robots already carry out many important jobs for us in factories, science labs and even in space. So what's next? Share your thoughts about the future of robots in a short piece of personal writing.

. . . .

Learning about language
Similes
Look at the following sentence from the first passage:

*His great iron head, shaped like a dustbin but **as big as a bedroom**, slowly turned to the right, slowly turned to the left.*

The phrase 'as big as a bedroom' tells us that the Iron Man's head must be enormous. By saying that it is similar in size to a bedroom, Ted Hughes creates the image of a truly gigantic giant. He has used a **simile**.

Similes compare two things that share similar features. A word such as **like** or **as** is used to help to make the comparison. For example,

*He ran **like** a cheetah.*

*Her face was as red **as** a ripe tomato.*

Similes can make your writing lively and enjoyable. But beware! Some similes are so well-known that they lose their effect and become **clichés**. For example:

as sick as a parrot   *as light as a feather*

It is more exciting for everyone if you can invent similes of your own. Don't forget that the two things you are comparing in the simile must be similar in some way.

Exercise 10.4 ✏

Write the following clichés and then a new simile of your own next to each one. Follow the example:

Example: *as flat as a pancake - as flat as a squashed hedgehog on a motorway*

1. as steady as a rock
2. as old as the hills
3. as safe as houses
4. as sick as a parrot
5. as fresh as a daisy
6. as light as a feather

Exercise 10.5 ✏

Write some new similes to fill in the gaps in the following sentences:

1. The day we won the lottery, we were as happy as _____.
2. My elder brother is as big as a _____.
3. When I heard that I had passed the exams, I felt as proud as a _____.
4. After such a heavy defeat, the team's spirits were as low as _____.
5. The cakes that Gran brought round are as hard as _____.
6. The class was as quiet as _____ when Mr Buckley went past.

Compound sentences

In Chapter 5 we looked at simple sentences. You will remember that for a sentence to make sense it needs a subject and verb. Some simple sentences have an object too.

Rosie   *bought*   *a new dress today.* *She*   *felt*   *very pleased.*

subject   **verb**   **object**   **subject**   **verb**

A **compound sentence** consists of two simple sentences joined together using words like **and, or** or **but**. The joining words are called **conjunctions**.

Rosie bought a new dress today and she felt very pleased.

Exercise 10.6 ✏

Join the following simple sentences together to make a compound sentence, using **and, or** or **but**. You will need to change the punctuation.

1. The tractor drove into the boggy field. It got stuck.

2. We were losing at half-time. We won in the end.

3. Are you coming with us? Are you staying at home?

4. Carolyn likes spiders. Her brother is frightened by them.

5. James ate all his sweets. Then he felt sick.

Exercise 10.7 ✏

Write the following compound sentences, filling in the gaps with an appropriate conjunction from the list below.

    so because while although as

1. I set off at eight o'clock _____ I did not want to be late.

2. I arrived at the match _____ the whistle blew for kick off.

3. I like Spain _____ I have not been there for years.

4. We had an awful time in Las Vegas _____ we never went there again.

5. Lazy David stared at the television _____ his mother hoovered around him.

Can you spell?
Adding the letters –ing

The author Ted Hughes often uses interesting and imaginative verbs and adjectives in his stories and poems. Look at the following lines from *The Iron Man*, for example:

All the separate pieces tumbled, scattered, crashing, bumping, clanging, down on to the rocky beach far below.

While the stars went on wheeling through the sky and the wind went on tugging at the grass on the cliff-top and the sea went on boiling and booming.

There are lots of **–ing** words here, and they sound wonderful when read aloud. Spelling these words is normally quite easy:

bump + **ing** = bump**ing**

boil + **ing** = boil**ing**

But there are other words that are more tricky, and they require some spelling changes to be made before **–ing** can be added. For example:

mov**e** becomes mov**ing** (the **e** disappears)

tak**e** becomes tak**ing** (the **e** disappears)

Rule number 1: If a verb ends in **e** then you must knock off the **e** before adding **–ing**.

Exercise 10.8 ✏

Add **–ing** to the following verbs. Some may require a spelling change to be made first.

1. smile

4. drive

2. jump

5. walk

3. live

Now look at the next example. It requires a different kind of spelling change.

jog becomes jogging (an extra g is added)
sit becomes sitting (an extra t is added)

The words **jog** and **sit** both end in a consonant. They also have short vowel sounds in them. Each word can be said quite quickly.

A word like **roam** or **boil** also ends in a consonant but the vowel sound is longer. So you do not need to add any extra letters. Say these words aloud and you will notice the difference: sit, jog, roam, boil.

Rule Number 2: When **–ing** is added to words with a short vowel sound and a consonant at the end, then the final consonant is usually doubled.

Exercise 10.9 ✏

Add **–ing** to the following words. Some of them have short vowel sounds and will need an extra letter to be added. Others will not. Say each one aloud first.

1. bat

2. feel

3. shut

4. moan

5. hit

Speaking and listening

1. Working in threes, re-enact the scene from *The Iron Man* by Ted Hughes. One person plays the role of the Iron Man by performing his final moments on the cliff-top and his fall. Another narrates the story. The third member of the group creates the various sound effects to accompany the story.

2. Working in pairs, re-enact the scene from the second passage. One person plays the part of the professor and the other performs the movements of the Iron Man. Try to imagine that you are actually on stage and the class is the audience.

3. How good are your listening skills? In pairs, take turns to pretend to be an obedient robot which moves when told to do so by the other person. Try to think of lots of small actions which the robot must do. Then speed up the commands and see if the robot can keep up!

4. Hot seating: Take turns to sit at the front of the class in the 'hot seat'. Imagine you are Clare Wojciechowski, or her father, from the second passage. Invite the rest of the class to ask you questions about how you felt that night, as you watched the strange robot demonstration.

· ·

Have you read?

These are all stories and poems by Ted Hughes.

The Iron Woman (Faber and Faber)
Collected Poems for Childhood (Faber and Faber)
How the Whale Became and Other Stories (Faber and Faber)
The Dreamfighter and Other Creation Tales (Faber and Faber)
The Mermaid's Purse (Faber and Faber)
Collected Stories for Younger Readers (Faber and Faber)
Ffangs the Vampire Bat and the Kiss of Truth (Faber Children's Books)

Other things to do...

- Use the Internet, books and magazines to find out more about what robots do for us today. You could begin by visiting the following websites, where you will find lots of interesting information:
www.arrickrobotics.com
www.bbc.co.uk/science/robots/techlab

- Read *The Iron Man* by Ted Hughes. Then write a short summary of the story. This is called a **synopsis**. You will need to mention the characters and the setting. Include just the main points of the plot. Try to fit the whole story into a page of writing.

- Write a story of your own about a time in the future when robots begin to take over the world. What will happen to us? Although we invented them, will humans eventually become the robots' prisoners?